THE EXPLOSION

THE EXPLOSION

Marxism and the French Upheaval

Henri Lefebvre

translated from the French by
Alfred Ehrenfeld

THE EXPLOSION
Henri Lefebvre

Published in agreement with Monthly Review Press, New York
for publication and sale only in the Indian Subcontinent
(India, Pakistan, Bangladesh, Nepal, Maldives,
Bhutan & Sri Lanka)

First Published in India, 2009

ISBN 978-93-5002-002-9

Published by
AAKAR BOOKS
28 E Pocket IV, Mayur Vihar Phase I, Delhi-110 091
Phone : 011-2279 5505 Telefax : 011-2279 5641
aakarbooks@gmail.com; www.aakarbooks.com

Printed at
Arpit Printographers
E-mail : arpitprinto@yahoo.com

Contents

Contents

1. Events and Situations

Events belie forecasts; to the extent that events are historic, they upset calculations. They may even overturn strategies that provided for their possible occurrence. Because of their conjunctural nature, events upset the structures which made them possible.

Forecasts and calculations are inevitably based on partial analyses and records, and cannot match the totality of events. In upsetting these forecasts, events reunite those analyses and conclusions which had become diffused. Movement flares up where it was least expected; it completely changes the situation, which now emerges from the mass of facts and evaluations under which it had been hidden. Essentials are thus cast up, especially those that are known and recognizable. Against this background are projected new elements of social life; these now become briefly visible in luminous transparency.

Events are always original, but they become reabsorbed into the general situation; and their particularities in no way exclude analyses, references, repetitions, and fresh starts. Nothing is absolutely virginal, not even the violence which considers itself "pure."

Although they are belittled during stagnant periods for the benefit of those who preserve stagnation—those who show contempt for history and are preoccupied with stability—events reactivate the movement of both thought and practice. They pull thinkers out of their comfortable seats and plunge them headlong into a wave of contradictions. Those who are obsessed with stability lose their smiling confidence and good humor. Good and bad conscience, ideological labels, and scraps of obsolete practices are swept up like refuse. Under the impact of events people and ideas are revealed for what they are.

Let the reader, however, look elsewhere for the irony, satire, cruel humor, and the pamphleteering vindictive tone which recent events will not fail to arouse in French writers. Here he will find only theory and analysis in an attempt to determine exactly what is new and what is certain in the midst of uncertainty. Such an analysis cannot be limited to a "point of view," whether economic, psychological or psychoanalytical, historical or sociological. It is essentially *political.*

2. On Marxist Thought

Certain intellectual fashions were prominent until recently. The experts in high-level political science talked only of *depoliticization.* Those who viewed this depoliticization as merely apparent, as a temporary effect of politics, were considered superficial and backward. The ideologues of the end of ideology regarded themselves as penetrating, profound, forward looking. Social classes in the Marxist sense? It had become so trite to refute their existence that students, weary of this platitude, demanded a new concept which could account for the fact that they viewed themselves as a class (youth, intellectual workers, etc.). There was endless discussion of whether Marx was "scientific"; attempts were made to divide the work of Marx into a good part (scientific, positive, absorbed or absorbable into modernized social sciences) and a bad part (backward, obsolete, partisan, negative, ideological). These interesting controversies provoked vigorous discussion between dogmatists and revisionists. An ideology of American origin, labeled either "pure" empiricism or "operational" rationality, was accepted as "scientificity." This, needless to say, was freely opposed to Marxist thought.

Another platitude gained currency: the forecasts of Marx are not being borne out. To know, after all, is to foresee. Religion? Philosophy? They have not disappeared as Marx had expected they would. The objection applies even more to the state, which Marx had predicted would wither away to be replaced by direct management and the administration of things. The world revolution, it was said, is not taking place. There may be mutation (a fashionable term) but it is not proceeding according to the outline drawn up by Marx; it is being propelled by technology and not by the class struggle or the drive of the productive forces as such. Historicity? History? They lose their relevance in an epoch in which the main problem is no longer control of development but rather the technical programming of the fruits of technology. Mental and social structures, which are immanent in historicity and transcend it, do not change. Alienation? It disappears in a society of abundance, leisure, and consumption. Only the fascination exercised by sex and death persists.

What remains of Marxism in such a perspective? An obsolete humanism, a sterile concern with past experiences, a myth of the whole man. Marx is regarded as the last great humanist. Working in the tradition of Diderot and Feuerbach he is supposed to have elaborated his theory of the "whole man" on the basis of a materialist anthropology. Humanism, however, becomes irrelevant in a society dominated by economic imperatives and technological compulsions. Was this not idealism from the outset? How is it possible to escape from practice dominated by the division of labor? The notion of a many-sided whole man has become meaningless. After catastrophically wrecking ideology, Marxist doctrine emerges briefly only to be swallowed up. The Marxist utopia is revealed as utopia—stimulating and delusive. As for Hegelian and Marxist dialectics, it dissipates itself in a rhetoric of history and a dramatization of experience. It contributes neither a method, a theory, nor a new rationality.

The humanist philosophy of Marx has had an impact, but it is obsolete, even for that part of science it once aided. Assimilated by a functioning rationality (the rational organization of society), it has been integrated into more mature sciences. The theory of contradictions in history and society is replaced for the better by the logic of coherence, the rigor of things. Viewed as the expression of an epoch, with all its aspirations and illusions, the work of Marx becomes a part of general culture. Once it is assimilated by this culture, it loses its virility and polemic scope. It has the same validity as the work of Plato, Descartes, Hegel—neither more nor less. It is a stage, a chapter in the history of thought. As for the complex of modern problems—growth, harmonization—here Marx contributes no solution, even if it is conceded that he has posed a few of these problems. In brief, Marxist thought is dated; it reflects the nineteenth century.

Such views were expressed by many people until recently. Today, at the end of May 1968, we must resist being carried to the other extreme. Yes, the proletarian Prometheus is rising again; his titanic figure is looming again. Yes, but has this Prometheus killed the vulture that was gnawing at his side? Can this Titan move the enormous rocks with his chains? If there is anything new, it is found in France (Europe) where the bourgeoisie hides behind technocracy and a veil of questions of technique. Who understands, who has correctly explained the relation between the bourgeoisie, and the experts aiming at power—if not at becoming a class? The question is not whether—and how—they can become part of the ruling councils of the state apparatus, but whether they have a specific strategy, and what kind. The conflict between capitalist and socialist society, between the exploiters and the exploited, has again become dominant. Yes, but the political regime in

France has placed renewed stress precisely on what it had been rejecting: parliamentary (therefore "bourgeois") democracy and, simultaneously, the class struggle.

Yes, but the ideology of consumption was not altogether ineffective, and youth escapes it only by means of revolt and the use of violence. People have lost the habit of participation and decision-making, except where consumers' goods are concerned. And if the very ambiguous terms "participation" and "integration" evoke so much interest, this does not mean that decision-making and participation have been restored. Neo-capitalism cannot be compared with the capitalism of fifty years ago. It is also true that Lenin had a historical orientation in a direction not foretold by Marx, but one which could not have been theoretically conceived except from a Marxist point of view: he demonstrated the revolutionary potential of the non-industrialized countries and sectors. It is therefore not in the industrialized countries with their concentrated proletarian populations that the process has assumed global dimensions.

Yes, but Lenin did not view the revolutionary potential of the proletariat in the highly industrialized countries as lost. Far from it. Moreover, the revolution in the "third world" does not follow a uniform course in Africa, Asia, or Latin America. Should the fragmentary experiences of this world in movement be incorporated into a unified theory and a revolutionary practice?

There is (perhaps) an option between the new roads to socialism particular to each country, and the worldwide road leading to the assault on the bourgeoisie. A worldwide picture cannot take into account the general law anticipated by Marx, formulated by Lenin, and verified over the past half century: *the law of uneven development.* This law, however, applies to socialist as well as capitalist countries, to industrialized countries as well as those yet to be industrialized, to countries experiencing growth as well as those that are (relatively or absolutely) stagnating. It applies not only to the end of the bourgeois and capitalist epoch, but also to the beginning of the socialist era. It enables us to conceive of a period of transition that may last centuries. Countries can be viewed from various aspects: uneven economic growth, uneven rationality of this growth, uneven quantitative growth and qualitative (social, that is including "cultural") development. The law of uneven development, moreover, applies to all sectors of social life: knowledge, technologies, sciences, art, daily life, the various sectors of production in its widest sense (including the production of knowledge and social relations) as well as the sectors of production in the narrow sense—i.e., the branches of industry. There are imbalances and gaps everywhere, which sharpen or veil (these two effects may be superimposed) the already existing contradictions and antagonisms.

What is the scope of this general law? At the moment, we are not obliged to examine the theoretical operation which enabled Lenin to develop and formulate it. In other words, the so-called "epistemological" question, that of the scientific standing of such a law, is not dealt with here. The theory of uneven development, incorporated into knowledge, cannot be reduced to an ideological instrument. What are its implications? It stipulates the emergence of *differences* neglected by the philosophy of world history and certain ideologies such as "economism," technocracy, etc. The Leninist law incorporates these differences into a general conception. Can it predict and act upon them? This is not clear. It shows the increasing complexity of the world over the past century but does not (as a law) make it possible to discover the solutions to the ensuing problems. Far from making the study of the concrete particularities of social development unnecessary for theory and action, it requires such study; it does so by an approach which is both empirical and conceptual. It thus corrects the abuses of dialectical thought viewed both as method and theory—dogmatic abuses for which Marx is in no way responsible.

Proceeding from the Leninist law, it is possible to state that institutions, art, culture, and the university do not develop at the same rhythm as material production or a given technology or a particular field of knowledge. It is even possible to conceive of the disintegration of a given "superstructural" sector which cannot establish or reestablish its links to a coherent context. In terms of dialectical logic, particulars are contained in the general formulation but cannot be deduced from it.

As for the contradiction between private ownership of the means of production and the social character of productive labor, considered basic by Marx, can we maintain that it has been resolved, that it can be relegated to a secondary place? Certainly not. Premature assertions and theorizing concerning this point and concerning the disappearance of classes and their struggles will fall, or have already fallen, into well-deserved discredit. Quite true, but ownership of the means of production is no longer what is was at the time of Marx. It has "socialized" itself, not because new people, whether managers or not, have access to it, but in a much more compelling manner.

Can we still speak of the ownership of an industrial enterprise by a capitalist or group constituted as a "corporation"? No. What is involved here is the entire complex of organizations and institutions engaged in management and decision-making. They are superimposed on the economic organizations proper, and constitute the foundation and instrument of what is called Power. They appear to constitute a system. The term "capitalist system" has not lost its meaning in the century that has elapsed since the appearance in 1867 of Volume I of *Capital.* Far from it. Its meaning has become more precise. It has become clearly and distinctly *political.* It is on this level that we can understand how it obstructs the *growth* of the forces of production and the *development* of society. If there is a system, this is certainly it.

But how coherent is it? This system raises questions, all the more so since the adherents of the system are obsessed with coherence, as they are with participation. They suspect that there are gaps and cracks in the System. The socialization of the means of production is posing new questions. Foremost is the question of *generalized self-management,* with all of its attendant problems. Can it be separated from other problems, can it be linked to a wider set of problems? This should be examined.

From the first chapter of *Capital,* i.e. the formal (axiomatic) theory of exchange value, to the final unfinished chapters, i.e. the exposition of capitalist society as a whole (distribution of total surplus-value and "income" in keeping with the structure of society), the theoretical structure elaborated by Marx remains solid. But it must be completed. And this is not so much in order to stress its scientific character and formal coherence, as to relate it to a concrete set of problems: the contemporary state in France and elsewhere; the relations between economic and political factors; the problems posed by growth and development, town and country, etc.

An important problem has arisen: the relation between the national and the global. Nation and nationality are engulfed by economic factors, by market and currency; this had been predicted by Marx. These areas are also flooded by the revolutionary movement, particularly that of the students. These areas, therefore, have not disappeared as political, ideological, "cultural," and social spheres. And the power of money, so forcefully denounced by Marx, has supposedly become stronger since his time! The extension of the "world of commodities" may cause surprise, but on the other hand the relation of money to political power is not clearly visible. Last point in this brief initial survey: the fetishism of gold, viewed by Marx both as the symbol and mainstay of the structure, has assumed global proportions. Gold has become the object of vast strategic operations. Does this spell its end or consecration? One does not exclude the other.

Following are some well-established basic points that may serve as a guide to reflection:

a. Marxist thought is the culmination of a process which went on for centuries, for thousands of years, and which is called "philosophy." Marxist thought starts out from both a radical critique of classical philosophy (from Plato to Hegel) and a radical critique of the fragmented sciences already elaborated or in the process of elaboration at the time of Marx: political economy, political theory proper, history, the study of ideologies, sociology. Marx initiated a new type of knowledge which does not abandon the notion of *totality*—a notion developed by the philosophical systems—but which incorporates it into the completion of the unfinished disciplines and simultaneously into the real movement of social practice; he did this by extending the notion of totality to include political action.

Without abandoning the results of analyses which fragment reality (natural, historical, social), Marx uncovered their rationality by reintegrating them into a world view. In constituting a revolutionary practice, he disperses ideologies. His thought thus moves back and forth between practice and theory. In its search for a total conception, this thought studies the transformations of the world and social life, but it is not the cause of these transformations. It is rather their reason: it is the expression and rigorous formulation of their *rationality*. It thus contributes to the transformation of rationality itself.

Ever since the rise of the industrial mode, societies have viewed and proclaimed themselves as rational. But these societies have not reached the final stage—indefinable in any case—of Reason. Every form of rationality, historically necessary yet insufficient, immediately gives rise to irrationality; this is a recurring contradiction that requires a solution which must always remain relative. Marxist thought contributes a *methodology* which one can refute only by separating practice from theory and theory from practice, and by attributing an absolute character to a relative and limited aspect of rationality. Such an attempt constitutes an ideology and becomes at once an object of Marxist criticism. The dialectical method cannot be reduced to a formal methodology, in any case. It is a methodology of action and thought as much as, and more than, a pure doctrine or system. In addition to the method there are concepts. These do not constitute a closed system but provide theoretical content and body for the method which, without them, would remain an empty form and a mere strategy of knowledge.

The methodology implies a theory, and therefore an approach different from the application of the abstract method to a given object. Is it necessary to cite a few of these concepts?

Alienation, the achievement of the freedom defined (inadequately) by philosophy, social classes and the struggle between classes, economic growth and social development, etc. As for the theory, it has a name: historical materialism. It involves an analysis of *levels* according to a double schema, horizontal and vertical. Viewed in terms of historical development, the relatively continuous growth of the forces of production proceeds along plateaus that mark the modes of production: slavery, feudalism, competitive capitalism, etc. And within the structure of a society, there are a *base* (technical and social division of labor), a *structure* (production and property relations) and *superstructures* (institutions and ideologies). According to the dialectical method which makes their elaboration possible these two schematic outlines are not unrelated, nor do they constitute a juxtaposition of two discrete spheres or dimensions. Within each structure elaborated on a given level, whether viewed historically or in terms of the architecture of society, a process of "destructuration" is at work.

Can this dialectic developmental process come to a halt? Marx and Lenin answered this question in the negative. More than one Marxist, however, has viewed the power of the state or ideology or money as capable of arresting the historical process. It is this view which in substance underlies "revisionism," a label that has been so abused that it has lost all meaning. Dogmatism has always opposed and still opposes revisionism but, by viewing thought and institutions statically, dogmatism always loses the argument to its opponent.

b. Both a theory of historicity and a leavening agent of history, Marxist theory contributes to history-making. This means essentially that it accelerates and masters the developmental process. Marxist thought consequently has a century-old history and its own historicity has a dialectic character. It has been enriched and impoverished, it has at times regressed, it has developed unevenly, it has had new and more or less well-elaborated experiences. Marx declared that competitive capitalism would be destroyed under the double impact of the proletariat and the concentration of capital. This has in fact happened. Marx, however, did not foresee that capitalist relations and the bourgeois class would survive the destruction of free competitive capitalism. He could not anticipate the flexibility and adaptive powers of these relations, and this in spite of his stipulation that capitalism had inherent limits and that the bourgeois class would continue to exist as long as it could contribute to the growth of the forces of production. It was inconceivable at that time that bourgeois society, through the mediation of scientific knowledge and intellectual labor, could partially absorb dialectic thought (while at the same time rejecting it as radically critical thought) and utilize it in organizing society and culture. Nor could it be foreseen that critical and revolutionary Marxism would be transformed into the ideological superstructure of socialist countries. Neither Marx, Engels, nor Lenin could anticipate a time when it would become necessary literally to reconstruct the method and the theory, and that any attempt, however infected with dogmatism, to move in that direction would have wide-ranging implications. For Marx, knowledge excludes ideology, for the sole reason that the historical and dialectic theory of ideologies spells their end. This results from a theoretical revolution which is inseparable from the practical economic and social revolution. The terms "scientific ideology" or "Marxist ideology," so freely used in recent decades, would have been meaningless to Marx. Everyone knows that he called himself a non-Marxist at the end of his life.

As for the double schematic outline mentioned earlier, it attributes considerable importance to the technological and social division of labor. This remains valid but does not obviate the study of recent phenomena. The extreme fragmentation of intellectual and productive labor (in spite of the tendencies toward the reconstitution of an overall unity on new foundations), and the importance of a technology tending to transform itself into an autonomous force, have mingled the technological and social divisions of labor to such an extent that it has become difficult to separate them analytically. This is apparent in non-productive but socially necessary forms of labor, as well as those which are immediately and materially productive. The direct intervention in production, and therefore in the division of labor, of types of knowledge that resemble ideologies makes analysis a delicate matter. This poses a set of problems that are partially new. They are our problems.

Marx elaborated an economic theory which also involves a critique of political economy. Not only of capitalist economy but of all political economy, characterized as the distribution of non-abundance and the forced extraction, under legal norms, of part of the social surplus product. Economism has long represented itself as Marxist, even though it is a debasement of Marxism. Marx never affirmed absolute causality or determinism. The economic factor can have priority only in capitalist relations of production. The theory of the general crisis of these relations is scattered throughout the work of Marx. Although he stressed the importance of the economic factor in the crisis of capitalist society, he did not reduce this crisis to its economic aspect or establish an immediate causal link between economic crisis and political crisis. Neither did he establish quantitative economic growth alone as the objective and meaning of socialism. In this connection, Marx holds that there exists a market (already complex: a market of commodities destined partially for consumption and partially for production or reproduction in the full sense of the word—labor market—capital market—exchange of those goods which today are called "cultural"). This market is governed by a general law, that of exchange value, which, until the advent of socialism, blindly distributes the productive forces among the sectors and branches of production, in accordance with the requirements and compulsions of society (which under capitalism is governed by class interests).

What then is the task of scientific economy in its practical aspects? To control the market, and utilize to this end the law of value. This tends today to be accomplished very unevenly in different societies, by means ranging from authoritarian planning to the manipulation of people, things, currency, money. The economy, however, constitutes only the "base" of society, a base which is necessary but not sufficient. A society cannot be reduced to its economic base or social structures. It includes superstructures as well. It requires not only institutions but also "values" and ideas, bodies of knowledge, ethics and esthetics. These terms are not found in Marx and their meaning is perhaps not quite precise. They nonetheless convey the fact that for Marx every society is a totality.

The dispersal and deterioration of Marxist thought into *economism* is completed by the related distortion of *philosophism.* This philosophy, officially called "dialectical materialism," has been frozen into dogmatism. Restoring the thought of Marx in its totality and enabling it to cope with new situations and problems means primarily ending this fragmentation. This fragmentation, however, has causes and reasons which are also historical. The theoretical revolution initiated by Marx continues, regardless of whether or not it is called "cultural."

Classical liberal humanism was never more than an ideology. The "man" of this humanism has long since died; certain ideologues today are passionately preoccupied with a corpse. As for the new humanism, that of Marx, it must be elaborated as theory and achieved in practice. Marxist thought, that of Marx and Lenin, has fixed several periods and stages along this road. First, *control of history*: men must cease making their history without knowing how; knowledge must guide these blind forces in the light of the politically conscious action of the working class. Second, or at the same time, *control of the market* (by utilizing its law, the law of value). Third, *the appropriation of the world*, of life and its desires, of space and time, the mastery by man of his own nature and life.

This road is by no means a direct highway. "Men" are still the victims of their history, wars and repressions. "Man" has hardly emerged from the division of labor which fragments knowledge and culture. This is all too true. The alternatives, however, are clear: either nihilism, or a renewed humanism. As for culture, we should be pleased to see it permeated by the thought and work of Marx, but on condition that it not be subjected to the fragmentation of knowledge and the dissolution of the "cultural." It must become a ferment and nucleus, it must reintegrate the rational and the real which have been dissociated, it must gather up the dispersed and inverted elements of rationality—this is the task. The proclamation of an eternal unity of the rational and the real was the illusion of philosophy. The achievement of this unity was and remains the task of dialectical reason. Each proclamation of unity was followed by dissociations and mixtures of ideology and science. Hence the need for a higher rationality.

In short, Marx's work is necessary but not sufficient to enable us to understand our time, grasp events, and, if possible, guide them. This is nothing new, but it is worth recalling.

3. On the Need for Theory

It is not too late to revert to the subject of Herbert Marcuse and his brief stay in Paris in May 1968. When he arrived at the beginning of a turbulent week, he could not know that the theoretical and practical situation would change in France and perhaps elsewhere. He was still unaware of the maneuvering his name and prestige were soon to inspire.

An international symposium held at UNESCO tried to drown Marxist thought once and for all in academicism. Marx and his work were mummified at a solemn memorial ceremony. At this official gathering, Marxists from all over the world competed for "scientificity" and appropriated from the works of Marx whatever suited them. Not satisfied with mummification, they performed autopsies, dissected the corpse and put it together again. Marcuse by his presence helped to justify this international act of appropriation, and to underwrite the incorporation of Marxism into "scientificity." And yet he had shown in *One-Dimensional Man* how and why the rationality of the industrial era, constituted as an apparently neutral and objective body, adapts itself to the existing order, contributes to its formation, legitimatizes and consolidates it! Implied in Marcuse's theses is the conclusion that the time may come when knowledge will shatter this ideology which simulates pure knowledge—a mixture of irrationality and would-be absolute reason. Does Marcuse's thinking point to such a future new, irrevocable stage? One would think so. Marcuse himself does not know.

During those same days the students began to move. Viewed symbolically, the course taken by this movement soon came to resemble a battle-torn street. The movement left ideological rubble in its wake. That burned-out shell? It looks like official Marxism, but is no longer in the least attractive. Those various objects? They are structures, now become unrecognizable. What do the students remember of prevailing structuralism? That pure violence alone can smash those renowned structures which they had been told were objects of pure science. Humanism? It provokes laughter. Technocracy? Fists are clenched. The students have rejected ideologies; this is one of the meanings of their struggle. Do they want to do away with all ideology? No. What is involved is not "de-ideologization," but the expression of an intense need for theory. Those who are beginning to move want a new theory; they want to participate in its elaboration for their own use. They are asked to accept Marcuse as "master thinker" even though they reject master thinkers and assert that thought has no masters. What are the students presented with at the very time they are discovering and widening cracks in the social structure? The theory of a closed society.

For French readers two books stand out in Herbert Marcuse's work: *Eros and Civilization* (1955, Fr. ed. 1966) and *One-Dimensional Man* (1964, Fr. ed. 1968). In order to understand the latter work, which bears the subtitle "Studies in the Ideology of Advanced Industrial Society," one must refer to the former, for the author, in the interval between the two, has modified his thinking. His critique of contemporary society has become sharper and more pessimistic.

In Herbert Marcuse's view, preoccupation with productivity, by opposing the "pleasure principle," tends to become identified with the Freudian reality principle. By thus producing a coincidence between individual and social needs, productivity becomes an end in itself (see *Eros and Civilization*, p. 141.) The organization of output and profitability permeates the whole of life. Free time—the time of freedom—comes to be sold like labor time in exchange for consumers' goods, durable or other. Whereas for Marx the productive individual participates in the creative power of society by transforming material nature, Marcuse views this "producer" as a kind of informer and spy to whom desire—the profound and truly creative Eros—freely surrenders itself. In addition, the individual in his capacity as consumer also betrays his basic desire and turns away from it. This Eros therefore tries to find a way out and liberate itself; it does this by disavowing the myth of Prometheus, the hero of labor. The myths of Orpheus and Narcissus mark the stages along the road of liberation (development of sexuality on the esthetic and even ethical levels, apprehension of space and time in terms of erotic "values" and in a context of non-repressive sublimation).

This perspective or "project" of eroticizing the whole life by effecting a break with libidinal functionalization and localization of desire—this is what is most interesting in Marcuse. To this should be added the idea of a junction of the erotic and political in the youth. Marcuse still sees a way out, an opening, for the creative Eros. His thinking deals with the relation between individual and society. In *Eros and Civilization* social control over the individual is formulated in psychoanalytic terms: censorship or rather "introjection" by the individual of social, ideological, and political solicitations. A particularly interesting aspect of this work is Marcuse's violent attack on what he calls "revisionism" in psychoanalysis. Freud in his view was and remains a liberator. Freud's investigations, which aimed at the dissolution of the repressive powers internalized by the individual, were transformed into an apology for repression. This deviation of psychoanalysis changes it into a technique of integration, for it is integration which is hailed as a cure for neuroses!

One-Dimensional Man carries the analysis of social control much further; the theory becomes sociological. "Industrial society," whatever its forms, institutions, and ideology, practices a policy of integration with increasingly powerful means (p. 17). Technology cannot be viewed as neutral: the transformation of nature becomes the prop, context, and instrument of domination. In this "advanced industrial society" the rational and irrational are telescoped, each changes into the other. The absurd and irrational are transformed into rationality, while there is at the same time simultaneous growth of the means of destruction and productive capacity. The "object-world"— the world of automobiles and highways, industrial and household goods—invades body and thought with the result that its alienated existence absorbs the alienated "subject." What becomes of the dimension proper to the mind—that of criticism, refusal, negation? It withers and disappears. The one-dimensional rationality of the "system" is supported by scientific thought, whether called conceptual and operational or empirical and positive. The margin of freedom grows narrower; the distance between the established order and critical thought contracts relentlessly. Magic and science, life and death, joy and misery merge on technical and political grounds (p. 248).

In short, Marcuse shows the restrictive or rather reductive

character of all philosophical, political, administrative, scientific activities (even though he does not express this thesis very clearly: the important concept of *reduction* is not made explicit by Marcuse and it is in France that it was formulated). These partial activities are part of a vast discourse which tends to become closed and to close society. To *reduce* means not only to simplify, schematize, dogmatize, and classify. It means also to arrest and to fix, to change the total into the partial while yet laying claim to totality through extrapolation; it means to transform totality into a closed circle. It means finally to abolish, through the use of logic—without solving the conflicts and the awareness of contradictions—an (ideologized) form of rational thought and productivist, technical action. How can this reductive and fragmentary practice expect at the same time to be able to *integrate?*

According to Marcuse social cohesion is the chief concern of power supported by an ideological rationality which embraces the whole of society. Repression alone (whether open or insinuated) maintains the coherence of this mass of reductive activities and disconnected objects. What are the results of this situation? The regulatory elements of Reason gain the upper hand. They dispel the negative elements that from the beginning of Western philosophy have posited two-dimensionality: the Logos and Eros, theoretical knowledge and erotic knowledge, both of which violate the limits of established reality. Whereas the Logos deteriorated into a "logic of gratification," the "scientific" mind has not ceased to weaken the dialectic notions (conflicts, contradictions, antagonisms) which had long been developed by philosophy in an attempt to elucidate the conflicting relations between "subject" and "object."

Marcuse must unquestionably be credited with calling

attention to a vast social phenomenon which is world-wide in scope, yet at a more "advanced" stage in certain countries. Science and scientific disciplines, or at least a mixture of bodies of knowledge and ideological interpretations, provide social structures with superstructures, while at the same time acting upon production and the productive forces. In Marcuse's view, linguistics plays a particularly dangerous role. Operating in the reified world of discourse, it purges thought and speech of contradictions and transgressions (p. 182). It consecrates a behaviorist object-world in which this dimension is already suppressed. This linguistic analysis mystifies the expressions of common everyday language by maintaining it in a repressive context. The elimination of negativity therefore gives it an effectiveness which is not positive but, paradoxically, negative. It eludes the prime requirement of philosophy: the meanings of daily speech must be elucidated by a language other than daily speech itself. This raises the problem of *metalanguage* (p. 195). Syntax, grammar, and vocabulary are political acts. As are science, technology, rationality. As is philosophy, which has the task of (theoretically) establishing the *possible*.

But can the *possible* (the openings) still be said to exist in this tightly closed world? Both opponents and oppositions are reduced or reintegrated, crushed or reclaimed. Society destroys or reclaims even the space of imagination. It holds out a world of mute objects, without subject, which lacks a practice that might guide it in another direction. "The reality of the laboring classes in advanced industrial society makes the Marxian 'proletariat' a mythological concept" (p. 189). There is even worse. Dialectical thought has been unable to resist the combined assaults of formalism and empiricism. "On theoretical as well as empirical grounds, the dialectical concept pronounces its own hopelessness" (p. 253). What can the philosopher do? He will avoid taking part in operations that mutilate universals—the Ego and the Subject, will and consciousness. Insisting on them also implies holding out possibilities. "The concept of beauty comprehends all the beauty not *yet* realized; the concept of freedom all the liberty not *yet* attained" (p. 214). But will philosophy be able to resolve the conflict between its two finalities: to establish the possible and to show the logic of the established order? Will it restore the rationality of *projects?* Will it support a new "ingression of freedom—not any freedom, but that of men who comprehend the given necessity as insufferable pain, and as unnecessary?" (p. 222). This is the problem of philosophy today. These men can belong only to minorities. "Underneath the conservative popular base is the substratum of the outcasts and outsiders" (p. 256). The philosopher and philosophy both stand on the side of the desperate.

In the last chapter of his book, Marcuse evokes the encounter between the most developed consciousness—that of the philosophers—and the most oppressed and exploited human forces. He mentions the *youth* only in the preface to the French edition, which he wrote in 1967. At the same time he stresses the new factors to which the war in Vietnam has given rise. For the first time the system faces forces that do not wage a competitive battle but who reject it "by struggling against it in its totality" (French edition, p. 12). This does not prevent Marcuse from placing even greater stress on the orientation of American capitalism toward a "closed society."

Such is the problem he poses. What image or conception of "industrial society" provides the kind of thought that will regain its critical faculty—or abandon it deliberately? What lies ahead of "us"? An impassable rock? A wall that will suddenly collapse under pressure? Gaps through which new forces will enter, pushing or pulling old forces, or leaving them behind? Is it not possible that (new and old) contradictions will cause the structure to crack, while authorities and ideologies try to fill in a few crevices?

Marcuse's theory carries the thesis of "reification" to its extreme conclusion and extends it from consciousness to the whole of social reality. There is no question of refuting it. Relentlessly, although without formal rigor, Marcuse heaps up his arguments. What does he show? An "industrial society" which is *structured* to such an extent that it is frozen into permanent immobility. Any movement within it is but illusion. The horizons are closed off. Only the desperate may attempt an assault. Herbert Marcuse *makes refutation impossible.* Irrefutable! What does this mean? Only *practice* can refute. If the movement of students and intellectuals enlarges a crevice, this means that the wall is cracking. And here we have an *action-critique* of Marcuse's thesis, at least as far as France and Europe are concerned. Since it can also be shown in other connections that current social phenomena do not fit in Marcuse's concepts and categories, this indicates that his analysis is inadequate. Theoretical criticism—the formulation of practice—will be continued, but on different ground. The question of acting "subjects," and of objects and projects (of the real and the possible) will be posed in new terms. And should knowledge become able to give form to spontaneity, the acceptable aspect of Marcuse's work will have been determined and delineated: that is, *its utopian function* during a certain period.

He pretends to universal relevance; but he speaks of little

else but "Western" society at the peak of its performance in North America. He describes only a developed society with very pronounced traits. Doesn't Marcuse's work still contain an implicit and ill-defined *reduction*—of *contestation** itself (including contestation in both theory and practice)? He postulates the control of production and the market in a highly advanced industrial country. From this he extrapolates the character of institutions and ideologies. He moves from the economic level to the political level, from the base to the superstructures. These superstructures, however, often appear fragile. The fact that they are, as Marcuse points out, supported by repression makes them all the more vulnerable, for "values" should be imposable without recourse to violence.

Herbert Marcuse—this criticism is not new—underestimates the contradictions in capitalist society; these are more skillfully suppressed in American society, more profound in Europe. Above all, he does not perceive the new contradictions. Is it not true, for example, that the relation between rapid technological change and established structures and superstructures tends to shake up these superstructures and become a source of conflict? Is there no conflict between the (ideologically expressed) need for stability, equilibrium, fixity, and a (latent) need for "creativity" and innovation even in American society? These conflicts, which undoubtedly produce cracks in this society, partially escape Marcuse. He limits social and political problems to organization of the market and industrial production. Impressed by American

---

*In traditional French and English usage this word has chiefly legal connotations; it expresses a challenge to a legal right or practice. The French meaning has recently been extended to express a total and continuous challenge to bourgeois society on all levels—political, economic, social, ideological. It is in this sense that the word is used throughout this book.—*Translator.*

efficiency in this area, he draws exaggerated conclusions from his observations. He neglects in particular the *problems of urbanization* and the new factors and contradictions they have produced in the United States and elsewhere.

It is too easy to criticize Marcuse for his lack of rigor. This would be an unfair reproach. Such a criticism is uncritical and belittles the relevant aspects of the analysis, under the pretext that Marcuse fails to provide a *formal* theoretical framework for his approach. He is rather unconcerned with epistemology. This enables him to criticize the social and ideological use of formal logic—the corrosion of dialectical thought by a distorted Logos—without having to confront the question of whether his rejection of formal logic does not also involve a rejection of an element or core of rationality. Similarly, while refuting an ideological use of linguistics, he does not come to grips with the problem he raises—the role of linguistics as such in science and "scientificity." Should a critical approach, however, be required to submit to categories which it does not share? If one imposes such a condition, the matter is quickly settled. One merely proceeds; and that is a dogmatic error.

4. The Revolutionary Crisis

The elements of Marx's theory are dispersed throughout his work. To unify them it is necessary to cease separating the young from the mature Marx, the economic concepts from the political concepts. The theory must be recaptured in its total movement.

Marx views the specifically economic crisis as merely shaking up the "base," as the point of impact of a decisive attack on property and the management of the means of production. The political crisis dissolves the superstructures of capitalist society, the structure erected on the base (technological and social division of labor) as well as the structures linked to it (production and property relations). Economic crisis is not revolutionary in itself. On the contrary. As analyzed and presented by Marx, economic crisis has a "purgative" function in capitalist society. It is absorbed by the cycle, which can now resume its course. It eliminates an excess of unproductive enterprises that are in a poor competitive position, due to the fact that their "production costs," as the capitalists put it, exceed the social average, which in turn is determined by the level of the productive forces, i.e. by the average productivity of the society in question and by the average organic composition of capital (ratio of constant capital invested to variable capital spent on wages). The economic crisis as such tends to restore the conditions of increased accumulation, favorable relations between the sectors of production (sector I: production of the means of production; sector II: production of consumers' goods). The reproduction of the relations of production resumes after a critical period. Shocks such as the introduction of new techniques, a strike wave, an increase in wages, may turn out to be beneficial to capitalism by forcing it to invest, by providing it with a widening market. Following a few inevitable disturbances, production and reproduction (including that of social relations) are resumed. Only the action-critique of superstructures (ideologies and institutions) transforms the economic crisis into general crisis, making it thus possible to transform social relations and the structures proper (production and property relations).

It cannot be sufficiently emphasized that it is impossible to reduce Marxist thought to economism. The specialized and fragmented "discipline" of political economy also plays a *reductive* role. It dissimulates the complexity of society viewed as a whole: production in the broad sense, reproduction of relations (and not merely production and reproduction of objects, instruments and goods)—a structure therefore that contains ideologies and institutions, "values" and a limited rationality. Even if the passage from one mode of production to another can be achieved only in the course of *growth* of the productive forces, this does not mean that social *development* does not have qualitative aspects which alone are decisive. That condition is necessary, but it does not suffice. As for revolutionary crisis, it is a total phenomenon which shakes society from base to superstructures; and the shake-up of the superstructures may react on the base as the result of an inverse shock wave.

Lenin transformed the theory of crisis in the light of new data. In his view, with the advent of *imperialism* bourgeois society and capitalism enter an irresolvable general crisis. Their strength is specious. On the economic level, the ruling and dominant bourgeoisie begins to organize; it passes from competitive capitalism to monopoly capitalism. Each monopoly attempts to extend the organizational forms elaborated for a particular company to the entire sector which it dominates. This involves capitalism in old and new contradictions. Even with the assistance of the state it cannot successfully plan the whole of production. Conflicts among the particular interests of monopolies prevent the social organization of the productive forces, even if these temporarily dominant interests are presented as "the general interest." The factor of competition reappears at a higher level; rather than disappear, it is amplified. Organizational capitalism does not become organized capitalism. On the contrary. By aggravating internal contradictions, the monopolies establish the conditions for an accelerated transition of bourgeois society to socialism and communism. In their attempts to organize production, they "socialize" capitalist property relations.

Violence spreads within and without. It spreads within each country dominated by "its" bourgeoisie; and it also spreads without, in the countries that are exploited and dominated by this same bourgeoisie. For imperialism aims at world domination. It cannot exist without exporting capital and importing cheap raw materials. But it does not confine itself to these economic requirements. Imperialism is political. Each imperialism has a strategy of its own which implies confrontations with other imperialisms. This does not exclude temporary alliances and economic-political agreements. At any given moment, the most powerful imperialism engages in a variety of actions—economic, political, military, and ideological. During the first half of this century it was Germany; since then, the United States. Each bourgeoisie comes into conflict with its own working class, with the exploited and oppressed colonial peoples, with other imperialist bourgeoisies. The tendencies toward coherent organization, therefore, are inevitably counteracted by the contradictions which they contain, provoke, and intensify. These tendencies cannot attain their goal. The superstructures of imperialism are marked by either lags and imbalances (uneven development) or the violence that is inherent in the military or police state. Imperialism has this essential character: it constitutes a transition toward something else (another society) but this transition is contained by violent means within the older framework of production and property relations.

With respect to revolutionary crisis, Lenin makes the following distinctions:

a. Objective factors inherent in the general crisis—the final stage of capitalism—which, however, manifest themselves unevenly (depending on countries and economic cycles, and social and political structures). In Lenin's view, it is not excluded that the productive forces may continue growing during the general crisis. He opposed the thesis of the collapse of capitalism (as a result of its inability to maintain and increase industrial production). In his view, this growth does not result in the elimination of the objective factors; these extend beyond the acute phases of depression and economic crisis. These objective factors contain contradictions that are more powerful than the successive episodic stages of prosperity and an active economy, recession, crisis, recovery. The difficulties which bourgeois society in its imperialist phase encounters in elaborating ideologies and institutions count among the objective factors.

b. Under these objective conditions, the complex subjective factors are essential. In a time of crisis, the morale and demoralization of the contending forces enter into the subjective factors. Among these, particular stress must be placed on the quantitative and qualitative maturity of the working class and on the existence and activity of a revolutionary party; and therefore also on theoretical knowledge. There can be no revolutionary situation without a revolutionary party, no revolutionary party without revolutionary theory. Lenin emphatically distinguished between two levels: on the one hand, spontaneity and revolutionary instinct of the masses; and, on the other, theoretical knowledge of the process and its total context, as elaborated by intellectuals (Marx, Engels). The political party has the task of uniting the two levels, of articulating them, so that theory may orient the spontaneity of the working class and its allies toward an understanding of society as a whole and its complete transformation from base to superstructures and from the social division of labor to the institutions; this includes a transformation of the property relations, which are the key to this process. According to Lenin, the party unites the objective and subjective factors. It is in the party and through its action that the subjective becomes objective, and the objective becomes subjective. Critical thought becomes active, negative changes into positive. The conditions for revolutionary change imply the neutralization of the middle classes, alliance of the proletariat with the peasants and part of the petty bourgeoisie, political isolation of the ruling big bourgeoisie and its bureaucratic and military state apparatus. Under these conditions revolutionary strategy has the greatest chances of success; in current language, it is optimal. This never means that the game can be considered won in advance. A conflict between social and political forces cannot be avoided, but the better prepared a revolution is, the less bloody it will be. The revolutionary crisis resulting from the conjunction of objective and subjective factors within the framework of general crisis erupts at weak points. It breaks the weakest links in the chain. This will suffice as a brief summary of Lenin's analysis of the crisis.

Have any new factors arisen in the past half-century, i.e. since Lenin's works and decisive actions? A great many. After the defeat of the Commune in 1871, Marx foresaw that the center of the movement would move eastward. Lenin declared later that the Asian masses would appear on the stage and become the subject of history. His theory of this movement is not that of Mao Tse-tung. During this half-century the revolutionary movement in the industrial countries was not immune to deterioration and failure. One of the factors making for deterioration is the institutional character assumed by Marxist thought itself and by the organizations inspired by it. The bureaucratization of thought and action, and of theory and practice, froze the forms which this movement assumed. It separated the component elements by uniting them into a political fiction. Political illusion maintains this separation through the fiction of a definitive, authoritarian, centralized unity. The movement, however, has not disappeared. On the contrary. It seeks new forms free from statism, capitalism, and state socialism. Control by a centralized political apparatus of production, of the means of production, economic and social organization, knowledge and ideology, art and the whole of life, no longer appears satisfactory, either in theory or practice.

During this period monopoly capitalism has not wasted its time. It has tried, not without effect, to resolve its contradictions, or at least to attenuate or suppress them. The attempt has been in vain. The spokesmen for imperialism have changed, imperialism has not. The most intelligent rulers of the capitalist countries (belonging to both winning and losing sides of the Second World War) have succeeded in getting out of the dead-end of colonialism. They even place their hopes in the internal market, in a "society of consumption." This has resulted in a curious "socialization" of society, accompanied by an equally curious "socialization" of property and the management of the means of production—a parody of socialism, a communitarian fiction with a capitalist content. This situation merits thorough critical study. Such a study indicates that not a single basic contradiction has been resolved. The objective factors of the revolutionary situation have in no way disappeared; they are latent and have been driven from consciousness by ideology and institutions, repression and violence. It is above all the subjective factors that were or are lacking—i.e. the consciousness that has been and is being assaulted and repressed.

During this same period these subjective factors, known collectively by the philosophical term "consciousness," became increasingly important. Blind self-regulation of the economy, which Marx analyzed within the social framework of competitive capitalism, gave way to increasingly conscious attempts at planning. Planning requires knowledge and means of action. The leaders of the neo-capitalist state lack especially the latter. They have partially assimilated a new rationality, but have not been able to translate it on the social plane. Indirect planning or (symptomatic) partial planning proved not entirely ineffective, but the system could neither define nor close itself. Under these circumstances it is the lags, distortions, imbalances—in brief, the results of uneven development—that become the objects of consciousness; they are superimposed on the basic contradictions which they partially veil. When they are latent, the contradictions operate deep below the surface. When they become visible, the differences invest the hidden conflicts with a reflective surface that must be taken into account, for it is in this area that thought and consciousness are activated, light is shed, and latent factors emerge. It would seem as if (established) society need only overtake lags and fill a few gaps. But this is an illusion. Although social reality has changed somewhat over the past century (certain contradictions have deepened), the appearance and surface of society have changed much more, as have the resulting illusions.

Under these conditions all technological activity and all specialized intellectual "disciplines" are revealed as both reduced and reductive. Consciousness loses the sense of totality, because totality is no longer present in reality. Where is this totality? What form and consistency does it have? Total reality appears as a mass of differences, imbalances, distortions. Fragmentary activities concentrate on a particular difference so as to be able to understand it (in vain, since comprehension of a difference requires a grasp of the whole); but they cannot act upon it (it can only be isolated, taken apart, treated separately). These fragmentary activities complete the process by which totality is emptied and vacated. This void is filled by ideologies and words; these constitute an aggregate which is maintained by repressive political power.

There is therefore an *increasing complexity* of society, but there are also unresolved *conflicts*. There are also highly developed technological divisions of labor, extreme fragmentation in all areas—in material production as well as nonmaterial production (bodies of knowledge, ideologies, art)—even though the need for and possibility of a total form manifest themselves (a total form based on the technology of automated production, and of the total process of exchange and production controlled by computers). This necessary base evidently does not suffice. Social division is superimposed on and mixes with the technological division of labor. Hierarchization, a corollary of bureaucratic management, poses new problems. Either automation and the use of computers become the political instruments of neo-capitalism in its attempts at "organization"; or this technological base makes it possible to effect a radical transformation, in the course of which the bureaucracy and its upper layer of technocrats will decline.

The problem today is that of social control of new technologies. Knowledge of society as a whole makes possible the achievement of a higher rationality which will manifest itself in this society. It is in this sense, and not in the narrow reduced and reductive sense, that knowledge becomes a social and productive force. It plays a role not only in the production of material goods—this is to reduce it to the economic level and economism—but also in the production and reproduction (in the broad Marxian sense) of social relations. This production becomes conscious and permeated by knowledge; but at the same time it becomes more exposed to ideologies which in turn are linked to strategies, state power, and decisions motivated or justified by the ideologies.

5. French Society in 1968

"State monopoly capital," "monopoly power," "fusion of bank and industrial capital into finance capital"—these and other formulations to be found in Lenin are not wrong. They do not represent a specific analysis of French reality. As generalizations, they are dated. The fusion of industrial and bank capital, for instance, was accomplished differently in Japan, the United States, and France. The process is *uneven* in different countries and sectors. A country where this fusion is more advanced or more skillfully achieved than elsewhere (e.g. in Japan) may provide a model, a loophole, a last chance for the leaders of other countries.

The schema of state monopoly capital is today too simple; in its own way it is reductive with respect to a complex reality and a new set of problems. Although the general crisis expounded by Lenin continues, new developments have since occurred that affect the content and form of his concepts. It is no longer possible to reduce problems to simple oppositions such as "capitalist society" and "socialist society," "exploiter" and "exploited," even though these oppositions are still meaningful.

It used to be intellectually fashionable to apply the term "revisionist" to all attempts to analyze the relation between state and society, under the pretext that at a certain period "revisionism" attacked the Marxist theory of the state. Today this theory is being confirmed, but in an unexpected manner. The state still places itself above society. This tendency—which Marx analyzed in connection with France (first in *The Eighteenth Brumaire of Louis Bonaparte*) although his strictly economic analyses were concerned chiefly with England—has become accentuated and perfected. The emergence of the state and the importance of state power had important consequences; first among these is the rise of a political system, a genuine political strategy—later to be called, in the terminology of Clausewitz, "absolute politics" or "the political absolute." At the same time the French state plunged, as it were, into the depths of the entire society. Marx's description of a monstrous structure based on "parcelled landed property" and a governmental, military, and bureaucratic apparatus forged for struggle against feudalism—this description must be modified and completed, even if it is still necessary to "free the majority of the French nation from the weight of tradition" by exposing "in all its purity the antagonism between state and society." This was done by the Commune in order to destroy the old machine. The state today is an economic power (the employer-state of several million productive workers—not only bureaucrats—together with state industrial capital and state finance capital). By controlling information which it cannot withhold, and by channeling scientific research and the university, this same state has immense ideological power.

The French state today stands above society but extends down to the base of this society. It is not at all confined to the superstructures but in a sense covers the whole of social life. It profoundly affects capitalist social relations, yet stands apart from these relations, guaranteeing and arbitrating them. Such a situation cannot fail to involve the French state in contradictions. What are the exact relations between the private and public sectors of the economy? The public sector is characterized by a limited rationality, by an attitude toward state organization broader than that of the private sector, which is limited to company-level rationality. The public sector acts as regulator and feed-back within the basically incoherent totality of this society. The public sector therefore is the favorite domain of technocracy. Its superior rationality implies conflict with a certain narrow-minded authoritarianism and therefore holds out the possibility of eventual democratic control.

There are those who would like to move the whole of society in the direction of socialism by strengthening the public sector through increased nationalization. Such measures would not change the relations between the state and society. How could the state escape the grip of the monopolies when it is a *political system* based on the monopolies, when it is itself—economically and administratively—monopolist? And yet, the conflict between the "collective" and "social," and "the individual" and "private" extends to very important sectors of French social life: medicine, education, urbanization, etc. Who understands this situation? Who can turn it to account? In what direction? These are some of the many questions being asked.

Power of the monopolies? State monopoly capital? Certainly, but such an analysis lacks depth. Can the power of the state be considered a mere function of the monopolies? Does it simply carry out their common strategy? Certainly not. State power alone holds the strategic initiative—this is an overall strategy which may be good or bad, which may be overcome by events or control these events. The monopolies—

or "oligopolies" as they are called in would-be scientific vocabulary—are certainly powerful, but each one occupies a particular sector. In spite of their tendency toward horizontal extension, they are vertical organizations—they do not in themselves constitute a system. They are not a system any more than the banks—each monopoly has its own bank or banks. Who is in charge of cohesion? The state power.

The great "companies" in France practice self-financing. This facilitates short-term and "regular" operations (exploitation of domestic and foreign markets, research of new forms of production) but hinders over-all cohesion. This cohesion is not assured by rational thinking (planning) but by the will of state power. State power can impose on every economic or social agency, and on each particular "company," the requirements of society—those of monopoly capital. In this sense, it can be defined not only as "power *of* the monopolies," but also, up to a point, as "power *over* the monopolies." Its capacity for strategic intervention is considerable; it is based on economic power (the "public sector") and on ideological power, which in turn is maintained by police and tanks. Could this powerful state confine itself to counteracting the tendency toward a falling rate of average profit in behalf of the capitalists? To be sure, it does encourage profits; it knows that a considerable portion of these profits is invested. In addition, it engages in management. It takes huge sums from the national income for its own operations (gold, nuclear force, etc.). Finally, it is actively involved in housing construction, city planning, urbanization. "Urbanism" is part of both ideology and the would-be rational practice of the state. State activity extends even to decentralization, which the country needs badly.

The state, up to a point, knows the country's needs, but the state which knows and represents is not the state which wills. The state which knows may sincerely desire decentralization; but the state which wills cannot decentralize. The state which knows desires (perhaps sincerely) participation so as to fill the void which it has itself created; the state which wills cannot bring about effective participation, since it makes all decisions itself. A final point. It cannot be viewed as a subject; it constitutes a set of dissociated functions within a fictitious unity.

This so-called personal power is actually the power of a section of the bourgeoisie. This section is competent, even devoted, and capable of pursuing a political strategy and a certain rationality. They help to make up the monster of state power, but they are not terrible monsters. Insofar as they can be understood by outsiders, they do not believe that the race for profits is an unmitigated blessing. They consider it rather a necessary evil, one factor in an over-all set of problems. They are engaged in management. What do they manage? The interests of certain individuals? No. They manage a country. This is their ideology, their outlook. It is limited, but relatively clear; it is limited by the bourgeois mind, but it is rational. This faction contributes to the cnlightenment of despotism, but without forcing it out of the shadows. It is a specialized informal political apparatus; it is an institution standing above institutions. The evil of this power derives from the fact that it is a malevolent force that destroys the social life surrounding it. Political life comes to consist of the hidden life of this power. It may even destroy the very conditions in which it functions. This destruction or self-destruction is inherent in its strategy, but it may escape power's vigilance. Such a power tends to destroy the separation of powers. It undermines the social and political institutions that might act as intermediaries between power and society. It destroys old distinctions and gives rise to new separations and previously unknown dissociations in society. Curious phenomena result from this situation, including the decomposition—a kind of premature withering away—of a State which is too strong, too big, megalomanic, megalocephalic, a monster of limited rationality. Intermediary organisms disappear; they are discredited, rejected from above as well as from below. They are reduced to a status of weak or strong *lobbies;* one of these is the working class lobby.

On the theoretical level it is not difficult to recognize here the separation of "political society" and "civil society" which Marx had criticized Hegel for dissimulating, and which Marxist critique restored in its true character. The state takes on the appearance of a political community, a society of citizens which is superior to the society of individuals. This is a political fiction; it corresponds to the legal fictions which it supports and by which it is supported. Every citizen—expected to know each and every law—can fully participate in the political community. He is expected to accept with full awareness the power of which he is supposed to be a full beneficiary. In fact, the political society deploys its hierarchy above (economic) civil society, while at the same time strengthening the hierarchic character of this civil society and the social relations implied by this society.

The Hegelian state still allowed for mediation between its hierarchic levels and distinct sectors. These mediations compensated for sovereign authority; they constituted the framework of society and included philosophy, art, law. They also included distinct bodies: the cities, the social "estates," and their specific organizations. The state which exists in France today differs from this model in that the intermediary organisms have practically disappeared—they have been either absorbed by the political apparatus or relegated into civil society as ordinary pressure groups. Between the political level and the level of civil society, there is a void. A political void, a social and ideological void. These groups, reduced to the role of passive members of non-political society, have not, for some time now entertained any *projects.* This word has been absorbed by philosophy and no longer has a practical content. These groups make proposals; they become objects of programs. They have ceased to be agents and political "subjects," they have become "subjects" of power. Hence the great obsessive myths propagated by state power itself: participation, integration.

On the practical level, it is not difficult to analyze this void, if we may say so, and describe the deterioration of the intermediary bodies. The specialized political apparatus, superimposed on the old "departments," in no way prevents the existence of an unofficial, far-flung, subterranean apparatus which manipulates collective organisms, gathers information, and transmits directives. Parliament—mediator between the nation and the executive power, a legislative power based on the classic separation of powers—has been stripped of its privileges. Important decisions have been made unilaterally shortly after an electoral consultation. They were made without prior debate in parliament, which adopted these measures by bloc vote on the basis of a text prepared by the specialized political apparatus. Many legislative texts, developed in principle by preparatory parliamentary commissions, are simply adopted following consultation with "specialists." These texts have amended the status of corporate bodies, inheritance and marriage laws, laws pertaining to the formation of "companies"; in brief, the civil code. Civil society consequently has been modified from above.

The third power, the judiciary, has been literally dismantled. Its independence, which had been maintained in the abstract, was in practice abandoned as a useless fiction. The nominal body of magistrates constitutes a kind of quasi-official body which directly serves the state power; it no longer has the ethical code or ideology of the old judiciary. As far as the regional assemblies are concerned—they were initiated as part of the tendency toward decentralization—they have no budgetary powers and are dominated by the prefects.

What a paradox France is! The country is full of talk of machines and computers, but its society is patterned on the order of the *ancien régime*. The third estate includes laborers (materially productive or other), workers, intellectuals, students, technicians, white-collar workers. This is a motley yet hierarchic order, situated within the general hierarchy. The clergy? It is a bureaucracy that includes a low clergy, high dignitaries and the technocrats. The new nobility? It consists of all those who gravitate around the centers of decision-making. Some use the power of money to achieve a crumb of power; others use power to achieve wealth.

This is a right-wing Hegelian state, but trimmer and more austere than the Hegelian state proper. It organizes, consecrates, and cements civil society while hovering above it. Insofar as it harbors theory and strategy—rather than a mixture of ideology and political empiricism—it is a form of neo-Hegelianism as viewed in high places through the eyes of Clausewitz.

It is thus that the state power has raised the question of power, and its centralized decisions the question of the centers of decision-making. How? By existing. By humiliating, through its mere existence, those who have not become adapted to it, even though they increasingly lose the habit of making decisions. By covering all things "as they are"—arranged and classified on official shelves—with the dust of boredom. These reflections belong to the domain of political psychology. What matters is that power has surrounded itself with a void —an ideological and social void, an official void vaster than the Place de la Concorde, a void that is vast as a world.

Why dwell on this void? Because it is into this stratosphere that the spontaneity of the movement was drawn and propelled. The spontaneous unconditioned nature of the confrontation suddenly replaced the unconditioned character of acceptance. Hence the events and their unexpected scope. What we have witnessed, and what analysis must explain, is the collapse of this society's *superstructures,* which were already eroded by use and abuse by the state power. They had already become dissociated in and by the illusory cohesion of the system. Along with the dissociation "state—civil society," other corresponding dissociations are maintained and supported. Thus the separation between trade-unionism viewed as an apolitical activity and as an economic structure that makes demands, and political activity proper reserved for politicians and specialized organisms. This dissociation is in one sense fictitious, but it is at the same time real, only too real. It is part of the political system. It is inherent in it—integrating and integrated within the very decomposition which results. It cannot be separated from other dichotomies: knowledge and action, theory and practice, technology and ideology work and thought, activity and passivity.

The dissociation between the political and non-political—both fictitious and real—is itself political. It is the instrument of a policy on which the state power and His Majesty's opposition agree. But here the secret is perhaps revealed—it is an open secret, the secret of cohesion within incoherence.

Drawn in by the void, spontaneity begins to fill it. It submerges dissociations, overcomes separations During those days the dichotomies between activity and passivity, between private life and social life, between the demands of daily life and those of political life, between leisure and work and the places associated with them, between spoken and written language, between action and knowledge—all these dichotomies disappeared in the streets, amphitheaters and factories. "Once the boundaries are crossed there are no more limits." Spontaneity needs an orientation. It requires a kind of thought which can understand it, which can guide it without stifling it. And yet, who is engaged in struggle in behalf of thought, knowledge and science? Theoreticians have more than once committed the error of not answering this question. There is a confrontation between the illusions of spontaneity and those of thought. The sea believes itself capable of rising up to the stars. Spontaneity acts like the elements: it occupies whatever empty space it can find, and sometimes it devastates this space. Thought offers another space, sometimes in vain; and other forms, sometimes to no avail.

It is quite understandable that in this paradoxical situation the authorities are feverishly engaged in filling the void they have created; this has been their only creative activity. They have eliminated all participation: Long live participation! They have monopolized decision-making: Long live the people who make decisions! They have discredited parliament: Long live parliamentary democracy! The centralized state is going to take charge of the forces that reject and, in essence, contest it. It will attempt this while at the same time forbidding contestation. Then action will change into agitation and spectacle, and this spectacle will change into spectacular agitation. The situation will also be droll: "Come, this way, not that way! Participate merrily, don't let up! Come, sing and dance!"

This is what they will say to those who would participate, sing and dance merrily, if these activities originated where they should: with themselves.

6. Three Tendencies

The ironic description of voids and vertical cleavages in French society in terms of three orders analogous to the three estates of the *ancien régime*, should not make us overlook the fact that the basic cleavages are horizontal—they are those of classes. Similarly, the ironic analysis of strategic intelligence and limited rationality should not veil the fact of power as political will. Situated above powers and social forces, power is will rather than intelligence or rationality.

From the point of view of political will, there are three tendencies in France; this is an additional cleavage which does not void the others. These tendencies are three, neither more or less.

a. *Archaic.* Its adherents are numerous, solid. This is the party of solidity, the old "right-thinking" party. They have a sane and simple vision of things as they are. For them there have been from time immemorial, good and evil, order and subversion, people with common sense and "ringleaders" preaching wicked ideas and hatching conspiracies. They have an unshakable conviction: order has eternal foundations and yet it is fragile. The identity of the real and the rational, represented by common sense and the moral order—how is it possible that anyone should wish to upset it? This is the secret of sin. The devil is ever watchful, the Evil One bides his time. These people have never engaged in politics. To be sure, they are representative. Of what? Common sense, certitudes, safe interests, an order that lies beyond life and death. Politics? An abomination. In fact, the archaic people bide their time. They always have something to avenge; they are always afraid. They are hesitant before the real, which they fear. They hesitate before action. When they do act, it is with malice. They become possessed, carried away. But not for long. They regain control of themselves and take possession of what has been done without them and against them. They are quite capable of grouping themselves into a party with a negative will, claiming and believing itself to be positive and representative of the truth—a truth based on bayonets. Reason and unreason are here confounded in the phenomenon of bourgeois good conscience.

b. *Modernist.* This tendency is much more interesting. They believe in mobility. They have a forceful and keen sense of imbalances and distortions (the multiform effects of uneven development) without, however, understanding the law which governs them. They are not aware of basic contradictions; these are beyond their spheres of understanding and action. They stay at the surface of phenomena. They want above all to answer the "challenge" of America, technology, the archaic tendency. Their notion of movement and reason is limited to a desire to catch up. Strong adherents of the rational —their own rationality—they want to seize the real and raise it to the level of the rational. They are Hegelians; they think in terms of "imperatives," "exigencies," and "compulsions." To adapt France to the general use of computers, to overcome lags—these are the principles of their political integrity.

They are not all alike but represent, as it were, a broad political spectrum. They unite the apparatuses that go under the name "spiritual families" by means of bureaucratic consecration and baptism. One family is close to the adherents of order; another—the upstarts—is still addicted to fancy verbiage and revolutionary rhetoric. In each of these families father and mother, or the heirs—girls and boys—do not share quite the same language or conduct. These details have little importance. What is important is that these people exist and view themselves as important. They are. They act. They act by themselves and through intermediaries. They are the appropriators *par excellence* of a movement which they have not set in motion; but they understand its relevance and want to be its interpreters. Their idea: the movement originates in various kinds of lags. They have little imagination and much ideology, but they are not aware of its ideological character. They include economists practicing economism, technocrats steeped in philosophism. Such as they are, they constitute the party of this movement, a party with its lower and upper limits: small and great reforms. The latter approach the threshold of revolutionary change; but with prudence, and the likelihood of retreat. In this movement-party (the expression should be understood in its most ironic sense) several groups have equal representation: the liberal center who would like merely to "adapt" the existing structures; the active wing of French capitalism intent on meeting the American challenge by modifying business and university structures—to modify the latter they seek to capitalize on the blows it has sustained; and finally there are the "Marxists"—they want to go a little further, toward the Soviet model, toward centralized state planning.

c. Finally there is the *possibilist* tendency. Stripped of any derogatory connotation, this term covers all those who viewed or view the "realm of possibilities" as still open. They are proponents of the potential rather than the real. They go therefore beyond the real and sometimes beyond the rational. They go so far as to proclaim the primacy of imagination over reason. They explore the realm of possibility and want to achieve some of these possibilities. Some of them want to achieve everything.

It is possible to imagine a dialogue between a young ardent "possibilist" and someone more practically oriented. Imaginary? Such a dialogue summarizes a thousand conversations.

A. (the possibilist): "The Revolution? It was possible. It was there. Power? The state? It had only to be seized. The state was crumbling. Ten million strikers! Who was not on strike?—even in the ministries, the state apparatus, among the police who were wavering. This had never happened before; it will never happen again. The peasants, in Brittany and elsewhere, were also waiting for their moment. But there was not only the strike, there was also creative, liberated activity at the base. The ferment of the movement gave rise to new relations. At the base. Bourgeois society was collapsing. What was lacking?"

B.: "That is the question. What was lacking?"

A.: "Nothing. Absolutely nothing. That's what makes me despair."

B.: "A great deal was lacking. Leadership. Direction. Theory. A will. A strategy."

A.: "The centers of production were occupied, so were

the centers of communication. What was there left to seize? A few palaces. What was missing? A few words. A declaration that the bourgeoisie had collapsed, that capitalism and profits were finished. Everything remained unchanged, except the ruling class and its representatives. We could have started out again the next day and tackled new problems: management, planning, the general direction of social life—in brief, the overall situation, the superstructures."

B.: "Yes, but . . ."

A.: "The attack was never made."

B.: "Those who could have given the order to attack did not want to give it. Those who wanted to make the attack were not in a position to give the order."

A.: "There was betrayal. A great historic betrayal by those who call themselves revolutionaries but have abandoned the revolution. How can you stay so calm? How can you keep this theoretical composure? How can you think so calmly? I am boiling over. I am trembling with indignation. I can understand a reformist. But to monopolize revolutionary language, to paralyze living forces—that is the greatest swindle of all time. There are corpses in our way. How can we get rid of them?"

B.: "Think. Those who claim to be revolutionary may have had good reasons for changing their viewpoint, for acting like sages. They know what they want. They want a legality which the bourgeoisie constantly violates and rejects after instituting it. You accuse them of betrayal. They accuse you of adventurism. You think they are holding on to an obsolete outlook. They think that you advocate action without theory and a storybook version of insurrection."

A.: "There is absolutely no excuse for saving the power structure and the established order when they were tottering.

I insist. By saving democracy, parliamentarism, and the very regime which they pretend to combat, they saved bourgeois society."

B.: "But what would replace them? Nationalizations? Better management of the economy? A higher rate of growth? Better distribution of national income? More coherent and developed planning? If reformism can be revolutionary, there is no need for a bloody attack in order to impose it. Within the framework of this democracy—the framework is ripe for it—the state and its apparatus will soon fall into the patient hands of the sages of the revolution. They will use it for the benefit of the people and of the working class. They will change it."

A.: "This is foolish and absurd! By then the bourgeoisie will have recovered. It will still be necessary to attack, but under much less favorable conditions—because this time the situation was formidable, unexpected, complete. The dictatorship of the proletariat over the bourgeoisie? The time was ripe, with the help of the entire people."

B.: "Yes, but why make the attack? In order to take power? To smash the state and its machinery? To substitute another state? What kind of state?"

A.: "To transform society. To change even the ways in which people live in society. Beneath its show of force the state was decaying. Why substitute another?"

B.: "To establish a similar society, only better?"

A.: "To change it basically. From top to bottom. From the bottom which was changing, to the top which should be destroyed, beheaded, democratized."

B.: "So for you it is a question not only of the economy of changing the economic system, of correct planning of growth?"

A.: "It is no longer a question of political economy. All institutions are involved. The whole of society. Human life."

B.: "You are moving fast."

A.: "In such a situation it is important to move fast. Society should not be subjected for long to this extraordinary dialectic—its own immobilization so that movement may pervade and reorganize it. Possibilities does not mean planning or growth. That is foolish reformism. Possibilities means something else altogether."

B.: "All right, it means direction, orientation. Toward what?"

A.: "That must be invented, created. New forms of social life. The movement proves itself by moving. We should have dug, opened, cleared the road to total revolution."

B.: "I think I understand. But I'd like you to be more precise."

A.: "I can't. This inventing and creating must be done within the movement, it must be inspired by the movement."

B.: "The others—those you criticize—hesitated. Those you accuse—not without cause—of protecting the established social structure against revolutionary audacity, have a thesis which you criticize harshly. They believe in it. They maintain it. They are logical. These revolutionaries have become logical and cautious. They view modern society as so complex that they hesitate before the responsibilities involved. All those delicate mechanisms—the market, banking, fiscal and financial systems!"

A.: "You can't be serious! Is that what stops you? Those delicate mechanisms will be destroyed, they will be reconstructed on a new basis. There were people on our side whom we would have liberated from the narrow confines which are stifling them, from all their specialized, bureaucratized tasks.

There are scholars, economists, financial experts, communications engineers. Think of how society could be consciously rebuilt from top to bottom with the help of science."

B.: "And the transition period? The period of construction?"

A.: "Everything would have begun to move the very next day."

B.: "As before?"

A.: "There would have been decisive changes at the top."

B.: "Don't you think that the entire society, making such a new start . . ."

A.: "On new foundations."

B.: "Careful! A new base or a new top? I insist on this. In making this new start, this society would again give rise to that on which and for which it came into existence—profit."

A.: "What are you driving at?"

B.: "My point is that a theory is needed. It seems to me that you accept science but are somewhat distrustful of theory. An over-all plan is needed. That is not easy. It cannot be improvised."

A.: "But revolution is a process."

B.: "Agreed."

A.: "The process was beginning."

B.: "It is still going on."

A.: "It was destroyed."

B.: "For the time being. Such a process cannot advance continually. And if it is really a revolutionary process, it cannot be destroyed in this manner. If the first revolution of the twentieth century has indeed begun, no obstacle or bend will divert it."

A.: "The movement would have produced its own forms of organization and action. Indissoluble forms."

B.: "You are right. How about the plan?"

A.: "No program ahead of the movement, or before it, without it, outside of it."

B.: "Agreed. But a concept that will orient the movement . . ."

A.: "Self-management! I repeat, self-management. Self. . ."

At this point the dialogue—a repetition of so many others—ends in turmoil. It ends at a crucial point: the new set of problems resulting from a crisis of institutions and from the reconstruction, not of a state, but of an entire society. We will return to this more than once. Let us keep this in abeyance. At this point some thoughts come to mind.

Is it not possible that political imagination may dissimulate political will—the political good will that ceases to be political insofar as it is good will? Starting point: contestation opens the field of the possible, as the philosophers put it. The boundary between the possible and the impossible is difficult to establish, but always easy to cross. Especially in the realm of the imaginary. Long live, therefore, the possible-impossible. Let us validate the movement by advancing. The possible? To change life! Certainly. But how? Those who want to define, locate, orient, establish stages and favorable moments appear to depreciate the profound mobilization of forces, the elemental *élan* that leaps from the depths toward the heights. There is indeed such a danger. And yet, if everything is possible, nothing is possible. Going to extremes of revolutionary romanticism, making the revolution within the revolution—these seem to flow naturally from movement, spontaneity and contestation. Is this true? Absolutely true? Does not such an attitude in its own way reduce the complexities of the set of problems involved? Does it not extrapolate from the (indispensable, profound, necessary) experience of partial groups or a single group—regardless of how important or decisive this group may be? Does the development of the revolutionary process not make it necessary for a given group ideology to overcome both itself and the ideologies of other groups participating in the movement? One may think and say so; but this is part of the problems at issue.

Before continuing the analysis, clarifying theory and attempting to provide an answer to these problems, we must return to a few essential notions. This temporary pause is not artificial. It is inherent in the "thing" under consideration, which is not a thing but its opposite—movement, events.

7. Contestation, Spontaneity, Violence

Such then is the nature of political space in France (the term "space" is meant to convey a static quality). There is a nucleus—state power and its apparatus. In its orbit move a few satellites and a few hard particles—they are instruments of this power, the means by which it exercises influence and control. This space is governed by an ideology or perhaps even a theory. Clausewitz had a concept of absolute war or an absolute concept of war (in its essence) which is the criterion for the evaluation of relative situations and strategies. France has similarly witnessed the development of a concept of absolute politics, which views the economic factor as no more than a means. Gone is the traditional notion of "politics first." Much more is now involved. A notion of highly developed political strategy has come to prevail. Stopgap measures and short-term tactics are obsolete. Strategy has gradually become essential. A political measure now has several levels and aims, including a perspective on the subsequent stages.

This state power confronts another center of power—a second apparatus with its own orbit, satellites, and means of action. This second nucleus shares the same notion of a political absolute—a notion based on Lenin and Stalin (therefore also on Hegel and Clausewitz). These two centers of power confront each other. But they are not symmetrical or homologous. Their strategies differ but overlap—on both sides there are men identified with institutions and institutions identified with men. To what extent may this be called dual power? For the time being the question is premature; the problem raised by this confrontation is not important. What is of interest is the void surrounding them—the ideological and political void which pure power, pure state power, creates around itself.

This void was filled by *contestation*. The original character of the concept and practice of contestation has not yet been fully explained and formulated. Contestation emerged out of this void; its aim is to link economic factors (including economic demands) with politics (as established in a context of the absolute at the seemingly inaccessible top state level). When institutions and men merge, when authority does away with legitimacy because it has itself become the criterion of legitimacy—under such conditions, how can "subjects" express themselves? How can they invoke their status as "subjects" so as to cease being "objects" of political strategy and again become effective subjects? How can they make themselves heard except by finding a new field of activity?

Contestation replaces the social and political mediations by which the demands were raised to an all-inclusive political level. Contestation is directed against institutions and individuals identified with institutions. It supersedes traditional separations and fragmentations. The "subject" is no longer a mere individual citizen—father or son, underling or overlord. He no longer confronts persons in their official capacities, in their private capacities, in their capacities as private individuals with daily lives or social activities.

Contestation moves from totality to totality. The majority of those who hoped for a movement, without assuming that the established structures would be paralyzed, expected it to originate in a "strong sector" of society subjected to strong pressures. The theory of the "new working class," for instance, viewed the technicians and skilled workers in the technologically developed industries as the initiators and vanguard of social transformation. This group—quantitatively weak but qualitatively effective—was to overcome the gap between strictly economic demands and the will to management and participation. Revolutionary reformism also looked to a strategy to be elaborated on the basis of industrial organization and an intervention that would politicize economic planning. As far as the students are concerned, such a perspective might have anticipated a movement originating with students specializing in the sciences—those who would shortly be involved in production.

But the movement did not start in this manner. Not, at least, in France. It was born among the students of the Faculty of Letters, especially the social science students. The students in general and the social science students in particular appear privileged, but they face practical and intellectual difficulties: lack of employment opportunities and acute awareness of a static social practice which offers no perspective or possibilities. The movement originated in a social void. This was not just any void—it was marked, as it were, by gradations and delineations. In Lenin's view, the weakest link in the chain maintained by authority, in the deceptively coherent chain of the superstructures, breaks not only on a global level, but also within a given society. This movement at first had a negative character. The void for these students consisted not only of a lack of opportunities or the absence of perspectives.

These lacks played a minor role. It would be crude to attribute the contestation to a "subversive" ideology. The students derive their sense of a marginal existence from actual social conditions which they feel justified in criticizing.

Contestation is first of all a refusal to be integrated, with full awareness of what integration entails with respect to humiliation and dissociation. Contestation is an all-inclusive, total rejection of experienced or anticipated forms of alienation. It is a deliberate refusal to be co-opted. The movement was born from negation and has a negative character; it is essentially *radical.* Contestation is by definition radical. It does not arise out of a partial "subject" or out of fragmentation. It derives its radical character from the fact that it originates in the depths, beneath the roots of organic, institutional social life—below the "base." Contestation thus brings to light its hidden origins; and it surges up from these depths to the political summits, which it also illuminates in rejecting them.

The youth may be said to define themselves by their "relation to the world" (J. Berque*) rather than by their age. The youth engaged in contestation are neither naive nor barbarian. This is an ultra-reactionary notion. They are not only enthusiastic and courageous, and even reckless—they are *anti-reductive.* They are intolerant of the reduced-reductive character of specialized activities, including specialized political organisms. They reject any perspective based on reductive views, whatever its claim to validity. Contestation is defined by this rejection, which may go so far as to encompass theory itself, for theoretical activity—the activity of thought engaged in analysis and exposition of totality—is

*Jacques Berque, a French sociologist and ethnologist, is a member of the faculty of the Collège de France.—*Translator.*

inevitably (in a dialectical sense) explicit and therefore specialized. Two factors come together: to the extent that knowledge of society tends toward totality, the science of society overcomes fragmentation and dissociation; and this knowledge supports and even legitimizes the spontaneity of the youth. Contestation rises up against the division of labor, the social consolidation of the technological division of labor into a bureaucratic hierarchy. The technological division of labor can be accepted as a form of coercion to be overcome; but the socially sanctioned and utilized division of labor is rejected. This raises problems. Contestation contemptuously and unequivocally rejects the ideology which views the passive act of consumption as conducive to happiness, and the purely visual preoccupation with pure spectacle as conducive to pleasure. What does it seek to substitute for this ideology? Activity, participation which is effective, continuous, permanent—participation which is both institutive and constitutive. This in turn leads to other problems.

Contestation arises out of a latent institutional crisis. It transforms this crisis into an open crisis which challenges hierarchies, centers of power, and the bureaucratization which has infected the entire society. This radical contestation must push its negative tasks to their conclusion; negativity must attack the formidable mass of what is viewed as "positive," "real" and established. It obstructs and undermines a rationality prematurely identified with the real and the possible. The illusory unity of political state and social hierarchy—based on separations which this unity legitimizes, on intolerable dissociations between daily and public life, thought and action, the production of material goods and the production of non-material goods (intellectual work, so-called "cultural" goods)—this fictitiously unitary structure becomes corroded at the base. It is precisely this very real void created by this illusory unity that is invaded by contestation. Contestation fills the hollow space from which it arises. It surges beyond the gap that lies between the realm of limited economic trade-union demands and the realm of politics, by rejecting the specialized political activity of political machines. In rejecting these limited economic demands, contestation reaches the level of politics by a dialectical process that reflects its own style: critical and theoretical contestation, contesting praxis, and the theoretical examination of this process.

Contestation arises spontaneously. It can be defined as spontaneity; it has the outlook and limits of spontaneity. There is of course no absolute spontaneity. The "savage" is an intellectual fiction. The explosion of spontaneity arises out of prior conditions.

In the course of a very famous discussion with Rosa Luxemburg, Lenin belittled spontaneity. Why? Because in his view a revolutionary movement requires an explicit connection between practice and theory, between class instincts and conceptual knowledge. Lenin regarded spontaneity as a subjective element and factor in a given situation. He did not consider or anticipate a case in which spontaneity would arise full-blown as an objective factor and as such intervene politically. In Lenin's view, the revolutionary party has the task of uncovering and grasping spontaneity from its very beginnings so as to orient and guide it toward political maturity. The campaign against spontaneity has since been waged in the name of science, in the name of insurrection viewed as a technique, and in the name of organization. By pushing this dogmatism too far—by considering spontaneity as devoid of any value and even as essentially irrational—

one abandons the attempt to understand its overt or hidden causes. In the name of a rationality that claims to be Marxist and dialectic even though it pretends to an absolute character, an explicit form of irrationality is designated as an enemy and thereby affirmed. But if knowledge does not accomplish its mission, if it fails to grasp emergent spontaneity, if it becomes dogmatic, systematized, institutionalized, then it is a failure, and it promotes confusion instead of direction.

Dogmatic illusions are being dissipated. If knowledge is necessary, if the waging of the struggle requires science and strategy, who is battling in behalf of science? No one. Who is assuming the slightest risk in behalf of strategy as an expression of rationality? No one. Ideology—insofar as there is ideology—is not knowledge; theory and practice undermine ideologies. But an ideology which is sometimes inherent in spontaneity may stimulate it. It should not be killed in the name of knowledge. Killing a spontaneous ideology instead of trying to understand it and guide it toward a practice which may overcome it at the right moment—neither too early nor too late—that is a mark of dogmatism.

Without spontaneity there would be neither event nor movement. Nothing would have happened. Power therefore regards spontaneity as the enemy. Spontaneity, however, is not a form of power. It requires conditions, it has a meaning.

In view of the fact that it exists by definition outside of any institutional framework, what is the meaning of spontaneity?

a. *A lag, or rather many lags.* Lags accumulate; a lag is a cumulative phenomenon—this fact is a curious conjunction. It is not only the university (ideology, pedagogy, content and form of teaching) which lags behind the needs of the market, material or non-material production, the technological and social division of labor. This is but one aspect of the conjunction. Wages also lag behind productivity and the "needs" being stimulated in the name of the ideology of consumption. Above all, reality lags behind possibility, consciousness lags behind itself (this lag can be overcome in one leap), and finally revolution lags behind itself (this lag is more difficult to overcome). What is involved therefore is the whole range of lags, distortions and disparities characteristic of French society, and of the modern world. The proponents of immobility and archaic traditions have not lived, thought, or acted in vain. Some of the (ideological and institutional) superstructures of society still lag behind the requirements of industrial production, organization, planning and programming. Top-level attempts are being made to overcome this lag—and this at the very moment when these "exigencies" are already obsolescent. A new lag is arising between the compulsions of industrial production and the urgencies of a developing urban society. Who is giving serious attention to these new disparities which contribute to the overall cumulative effect? Critical thought about the role of specialized political organisms, about ideologies and institutions, and about pervasive terrorism, must concern itself also with these facts. All these lags have resulted in a general deterioration of society and the state. But they have also produced conditions that enabled a marginal and apparently insignificant student movement to affect the whole range of institutions by unleashing spontaneity.

b. It was in the streets that the demonstrations took place. It was in the streets that spontaneity expressed itself—in an area of society not occupied by institutions. From there it spread to institutional areas. This characteristic of the movement indicates that partly new and original urban phenomena are already involved. The streets have become politicized—this fact points up the political void prevailing in the specialized areas. Social space has assumed new meaning. This entails new meaning. This entails risks. Political practice transferred to the streets sidesteps the (economic and social) practice which emanates from identifiable places. Hence the danger of new dissociations.

c. Spontaneity and the transformation of the streets into political arenas have led to the rebirth of the phenomenon and problem of *violence.* Violence is connected with spontaneity and therefore with contestation—with forces that are in search of orientation and can exist only by expressing themselves. History thus resumes its course—a history that appeared to have been arrested, fixed, dominated by power for its benefit. It may be useful here to recall the relation as well as the distinction between latent and open violence. Power may limit itself to latent violence. It prefers not to use its means of brutal intervention. Holding these means in reserve is part of a strategy elaborated long ago by Machiavelli. The regimes that used police and military repression on every occasion had not yet developed the concept of absolute politics. This concept views the use of force as necessary only when the adversary must be definitively crushed. Until then, partial intervention and threats entail the risk of establishing the adversary as a representative of the opposition. This must be allowed only under special circumstances. Latent violence, however, provokes a counter-violence which reveals it, which may impede it and force it to unmask itself in open attack. Violence may even wear itself out and be defeated by counter-violence. Under these conditions, the romanticism of pure violence may come to the fore. It implies a philosophy: the ontology of unconditional spontaneity, the metaphysics of violence. After a long period during which the class struggle was weakened by history and historicity, by peaceful co-existence, by stagnating social relations and "unconsciously" accumulated lags, the conjuncture of events is favorable to the rebirth of this philosophy. For the youth the "yé-yé" period is now followed by one of tragedy. The crumbling of the ideologies of equilibrium, growth and harmonization is accompanied by the temptation of a new absolute. Did the terrible cry, *Viva la muerte!* resound in the streets of Paris? By no means. It is to the honor of those who follow the black flag that they have never committed the lives of others—friends or enemies—without risking their own lives in total commitment. This honor and this will constitute a great danger for a "world" that has no honor and no will other than that of maintaining its own existence.

d. Deep-seated spontaneity is in fact not only a reaction to disparities and accumulated lags. It is also symptomatic of new contradictions superimposed on older contradictions that were veiled, blurred, *reduced,* but never resolved. Theoretical analysis must study and elucidate this dramatic and highly complex situation. It must do so by means of an instrument that is refined and sharpened by conjunctures and events—dialectical thought. This instrument appeared to have lost its edge. It *had* lost it. If dialectical analysis does not succeed in grasping the (old and new) elements in the situation, in explaining them in their totality, in providing them with meaning, then despair will gain the upper hand. Reliance on violence may lead to a rebirth of a tragic consciousness as much opposed to the dialectical conception of becoming as the dialectical conception was opposed to "structuralism," the ideology of immobility. In other words, a serious concern with spontaneity implies at the same time a delineation of spontaneity. This must be done in the name of a theory which pure spontaneity tends to ignore.

8. Strategies for Outflanking and the Outflanking of Strategies

The analysis of strategies leads to surprising results. A theoretical and conceptual effort, it deals with acts and with the connections between supposedly premeditated actions. It deals with power and its supposedly coherent measures. Power (i.e. state power) implies the potential or actual use of force. It also implies a mode of thought. Without thought, state power loses its capacity for action and disintegrates; plots, coups, and assassinations become inevitable. A mode of thought requires articulation and formulation. Power therefore presupposes the use of language. It is based on language insofar as language directs the use of force. This does not mean that power is nothing but language.

Strategic analysis entails the risk and possibility of an illusion; it may attribute a high degree of intelligence and political genius to the representatives of power. A measure taken empirically or pragmatically may be interpreted subsequently as a strategic decision. This is not a serious risk. A measure arrived at empirically becomes part of strategy—and strategy is the object of analysis.

Political strategy today has generally achieved a high degree of subtlety. It has long-term perspectives. This is not unconnected with the concept of "absolute politics." The adversary is often allowed to take the initiative in order that wavering allies and weakening friends may be reminded of one's indispensability. Measures taken by state power have a number of effects. The importance of a possible adversary may be enhanced by giving him wide publicity, by using this publicity as a diversion from the real problems, and by veiling the effects of the real forces on the real process. It is thus possible to select the adversary as well as the combat area and the stakes. It is widely known that the state power permitted the student movement to develop, even if it did not help it actively. Why? In order to shake up the "archaic" people and institutions, point up lags, and open the way for measures that might have overcome these lags in a desirable manner. The movement subsequently went beyond its original framework—thereby showing how dangerous such a strategic game can be.

Strategy has a two-fold character, even though the application of absolute politics gives it a certain unity. There is an apparent, public, and publicized strategy, and there is a strategy that is hidden and secret. The former—its public character does not exclude efficacy—is akin to tactics, but this is part of strategy. The latter—a long-term strategy—is never revealed; it appears only in statements and speeches intended to alert and impress so-called public opinion. The political content of these speeches must be distinguished from the content designed to promote publicity, propaganda, credibility, or terror.

All strategies give rise to forces that may cause these strategies to exceed their intended limits. These forces are within the realm of logistics and calculation; they can be anticipated. Strategy envisages their capture or destruction once they are uncovered. This entails new dangers. As in any strategic consideration, the strategist has a choice of two options—to attempt to minimize the possibilities open to the adversary or to attempt to maximize his own possibilities. No tactical or strategic operation is devoid of risks. Strategic projects and their analysis can be made only in terms of chance and probability. There are those who fear "adventure" to the point of rejecting it in the name of a situational logic or a situation reduced to logic—but they either have no strategy, or do not want a strategy, or conceal it behind this logic. The logic of strategies is not formal; it is a dialectical logic.

In order to understand strategy, it is necessary to ask a number of simple questions: "Who? How? Why?" The answer is never simple, for analysis must determine the real adversary as well as the real objectives. Whoever initiates a strategic operation on the level of absolute politics fixes upon an adversary whose strategy, it is feared, may be designed to outflank him and may itself be outflanked. By designating his adversary as "legal" he compels him to remain on the plane of legality; he thus retains the option of attacking him at a future time in the name of this legality. The real adversary is the sum total of the forces that threaten to outflank him. The fictitious adversary finds it necessary to watch his rear guard so as not to be outmaneuvered on the plane of legality. He enjoys at the same time a maneuverability which makes this surveillance possible. General attention can now be concentrated on the arena in which the political game is taking place. But the real action must be understood in terms of other factors—not only the streets but also the forces that threaten outflanking; these forces respect neither the game nor the rules of the game.

There is nothing new in the fact that the initiators of an action—those who foment and accomplish it—may be disavowed by those who capitalize on it. A new element arises from the fact that a strategy belongs to no one. Whoever can carry it out makes it his own. What is a strategy? It is a form. This form consists of the means of action and the instruments that make its execution possible. One political leader may conceive of a strategy without disposing of the necessary means; another may take over this strategy and carry it out because he has the means. During the period of history which began in 1933, a global strategy designed to achieve "independence, grandeur, prosperity" for France was perfectly conceivable. It was even necessary. Small-minded politicians were unable to accept this. They could not abandon the tactics of electoral politics at home and temporary alliances abroad. The present head of state in France then wrested the strategy from the opposition. Acting in the upper reaches of top-level politics, he neglected national realities and domestic problems to some extent.

What is he trying to do today, in May-June, 1968? To assume control of the only conceivable national strategy. His strategic virtuosity, inspired by the concept of "absolute politics," extends even to making use of the void which he has himself created. What does this involve? The reconstruction of social life. This requires an essential condition: the active *participation* of social groups (students, the youth, workers, technicians). If the opposition had elaborated a strategy, it would have advanced a program of generalized self-management instead of confining itself to improved planning or increased nationalization within the framework of the current state. The opposition therefore is to a certain extent disarmed and vulnerable.

The official strategy does not lack audacity. It even holds out the possibility of a third way (the famous "third way") between socialism and capitalism. It may be asked whether this strategy disposes of the means for achieving its end. For the state to fill the social void which it has itself created around the state apparatus, for the state to demand from the top what can come only from below—is this not the ultimate paradox of absolute politics?

9. On Dual Power

For its analysis of this situation, dialectical thought needs new terms that are well-defined yet capable of expressing volatile, uncertain elements. Power? Is it the power of a shadow or the shadow of a power? Certainly not. Those in power have ready access to the means of action. They dispose of specific mechanisms that activate real forces. But the specter of absolute politics which looms over Europe and the world and which has replaced the specter of communism to small advantage, has a somewhat unreal quality. It manifests all the aberrations of the will to power, all the juridical and political fictions associated with the state. It proclaims itself and has itself proclaimed at the very moment it has created a void of terror around itself. It is the whole of society that must be rebuilt; its superstructures—it is because of them that a society is a society and not a mere agglomerate—have become shaky and have at all times collapsed. The concept of absolute politics suggests to the men in power that power must and can be the basis for a reconstruction of this society. This is the delirium of a rationality which cannot accept its own limitations

In Lenin's view, dual power is characteristic of revolutionary situations. As one power declines, another rises. The Commune witnessed both the so-called Republican government and the Central Committee of the National Guard. In

1917 there was a center of power occupied by the adherents of Kerensky, and there were the Soviets. Can potential or real dual power be said to exist in France today (end of May, early June, 1968?) One might think so. There are on one side the bourgeoisie and its allies assembled under the flag of the Republic and liberty ("liberate our factories!") and on the other side the working class and its allies under the flag of democracy and liberties. This, however, is but appearance (with the reservation contained in the dialectical proposition that "every appearance contains a reality which may develop"). The two powers confronting each other are in fact but one—they are situated on the same terrain of legality, the established state, and the parliamentary game. This terrain is occupied by those who have the power to initiate action. Consequently the terrain of political action is occupied by two forces, but by one power.

To the men associated with institutions—the representatives of the state—dual power is inconceivable and intolerable. They hardly ever refer to it. If they spoke of it, they would empty the concept of its content. Not long ago Parliament appeared to be a symbol of the social and ideological void that surrounds politics; its debates were very disappointing in their lack of relevance. The second force, however, apparently wants to restore parliamentary life. It thereby risks dissimulating the void and masking the absence of intermediary organisms between the apparatus and the "base," and abandoning reactivated institutions to the "class" enemy. There appears to be a good deal of logic in this position. But this logic, unfortunately, may salvage the general logic of a system that has lost its coherence.

The most surprising characteristic of the situation in France during those "historic" hours was and still is the existence of a third force: contestation and spontaneity—the force of the streets. In a sense this power, which lies outside of state power, was and remains the most real and active power. To shake up a society, or rather to make its institutional crisis palpable—this can result only from effective power. Such power however, has difficulty in constituting and affirming itself as power. It is a concrete force which was first negative and then became positive due to the power of contestation and the movement. How can a movement based on negation become a power? How can it move from contestation to institution? The resumption of a spontaneity whose *élan* flows into the gaps and voids of society results in a delineation of the void. Spontaneity thus holds out a magnificent vision and possibility: the total reconstruction of society, a democracy permeated by the movement, based on a network of "base" organisms in which all interests, all aspirations and all liberties would be actively present (instead of being merely represented). This notion of a democracy rooted in the base is forcefully opposed to the notion of republic (public thing) managed and maintained at the top. Based on the partial decomposition and decline of the established state, it challenges the thesis of the democratic state.

What did Marx have to say about this? He held that democracy develops through a contradiction: democracy implies a state; but democracy also tends toward the elimination of the state, for otherwise it destroys itself. This raises the possibility of a restoration of social intermediaries and mediations in the vast social area that lies between the centers of absolute politics with their organisms and instruments of action, and the social practice rooted in the base. For the time being such a restoration may remain no more than possibility. Should this possibility be realized, however, there will have taken place a colossal movement, and a general strike whose political content will have been nipped in the bud. History will then have produced a revolutionary situation without revolution. The opening made in a wall that was already cracking will not have provided an outlet for the movement. The elimination of intermediary organisms will have vainly left the contending classes face to face, and the working class will again have been rejected as a class by the sovereign power and by the national state. Electoral and parliamentary tactics will have been temporarily replaced by strategy to no avail. The great ideologies of growth, economism, absolute politics, and the state, also will have been vainly shaken by the practitioners of contestation.

But is such a new void possible? Would it witness the reconstruction and reinstitution of dissociations and separations—between economic, social and political factors, between daily life and the spheres of culture and power, between passivity and the capacity for action? Will there be a rebirth of the ideology of consumption and the ideology of "non-ideology"? This appears impossible. It seems highly probable that the movement, after some regression, will be reborn, most likely elsewhere and in a different guise. The third force—which is in no way a "third way"—will give rise to projects, ideas, and a totally transformed social practice. Its intervention has already pointed up in practice the primary role of *consciousness,* so contemptuously accused of "subjectivity." Its task now is not only to occupy the areas of social void as well as some other areas, but also to fill "positively" the voids of consciousness and social reality itself. The task of the theoretician can hardly go beyond this analysis. He can do no more than indicate the tasks which social practice can accomplish.

10. On Self-Management

It need hardly be recalled that the concept and practice of self-management constitute an original answer to the problem of the socialization of the means of production posed by Marx, and that this concept and practice are unaffected by the difficulties which, since the time of Marx, have arisen with respect to authoritarian and centralized planning. It should perhaps be emphasized that there is nothing magical about self-management and that it is not a panacea. It has raised and still raises as many problems as it has resolved. Once posited in principle, it still needs to be "thought through" within the framework of a highly industrialized country and a world situation characterized by numerous new factors.

Self-management does not do away with the class struggle. It may stimulate it. Without self-management, participation becomes meaningless, makes various kinds of manipulation possible, and becomes an ideology. Self-management alone can make participation effective by including it in a process aiming at totality. Self-management raises a whole range of problems; so does participation. These are immense problems. The transformation of the entire social life of a complex society faces obstacles. Taken in isolation—i.e. divorced from the problems it raises and abstracted from a comprehensive theoretical project—self-management is but an empty slogan. It becomes empty when viewed out of context. In advancing it, the worshippers of full state economic control are playing with words.

The slogan of self-management arose spontaneously in the "empty" areas of social life—i.e. in the void created by the state—as the expression of a basic social need from which it cannot be isolated. It implies an all-inclusive project which, if made explicit, could fill the void. The social and political content of self-management must become strategy, or the project will fail.

The empty, dangerous slogan is that of "co-management." Co-management is incompatible with self-management. It does not come to grips with management, its challenge is confined in advance to the framework of management, it does not contest this framework. Pseudo-revolutionary reformism can do no more than streamline the same management within the same institutions and restore them with the aid of "interested parties." Self-management, however, has different consequences:

a. It makes a breach in the established network of decision-making centers which manage production and organize consumption without granting producers and consumers the slightest concrete freedom or participation in making genuine choices.

b. It involves a risk: there may take place a degeneration and recuperation especially in the already bastardized and distorted forms of "co-management." Within the framework of self-management itself, partial or local interests may come to dominate the general interests of society.

c. Self-management portends the surge through the breach of a process extending over the whole of society. It would be wrong to confine this process to the management of economic affairs (enterprises, branches of industry, etc.). Self-management implies a social *pedagogy*. It presupposes a new social practice at all stages and levels. This process involves the shattering of bureaucracy and centralized state management. The process encounters obstacles: the market and control of the market, over-all problems relating to investment, etc. There is no dilemma or option between state centralization and a decentralization which favors the partial and local over the whole. Such a dilemma is part of the ideology of absolute politics (of a state and political absolute). These are not insurmountable obstacles or unsolvable problems. They are nonetheless real. The process of self-management—the social practice and the theory of this practice—implies the establishment at the base of a complex network of active bodies. Practice and theory modify the classic concept (in formal democracy) of representation and representativeness. The many interests of the base must be present, and not merely "represented" or handed over to delegates who become divorced from the base. Effective self-management and participation cannot be separated from a "system" of direct democracy akin more to a continuous and continuously renewed movement deriving its organizational capacities from within itself, than to a formal "system." Relations change at all levels. The old relations between those who are active and those who are passive, between the rulers and the ruled, between decisions and frustrations, between subjects and objects—all these are dissolved. This may give rise to disorder, the emphasis on unfettered speech may collide with the jargon of bureaucratic documents, but these are serious inconveniences only for the supporters of the established order. As far as overall management is concerned, here new technologies can intervene. Automation at the base of the productive forces, the utilization of electronic devices such as computers capable of providing decentralized management with a continuous flow of information—these new technologies create new possibilities. But on condition that they be used to promote the withering of state and bureaucracy, and not to strengthen institutions technocratically.

Not the least of the dangers threatening self-management as a *process* is the reliance on corporate interests—the interests of unity of production or of a branch of production (taking this term in its wider sense so as to include the production of intellectual work and "services"). It may be thought that particular interests are being transcended, when in fact they are being maintained. The university which regards itself as decisive in transforming society because it can occupy an essential role in it, practices neo-corporatism. This applies equally to architects, urbanists, magistrates, judiciary power, technicians, information specialists, etc. Since all specialized activity is reduced-reductive, it must have recourse to incessant self-criticism; this is a corollary and complement of self-management. Self-management implies self-criticism and continuous active scrutiny of the relations between the functional and structural limits of a self-managing entity and society as a whole.

As for co-management and autonomy, their implications are evident. In particular the autonomy of universities, faculties and departments may leave them in the hands of "archaic" elements and subordinate them blindly to the exigencies of the market, deprive them of critical activity, and drive pedagogy and knowledge into a state of immobility more pronounced than ever.

A discussion of self-management is certainly the proper place to recall the importance of everyday life. The revolutionary process begins by shaking up the condition of everyday life and ends by restoring it. What is it that shatters and submerges this condition? It is the active subversion of the conditions that maintain it by divorcing it from "extraordinary" possibilities. The subversion undermines previously mentioned dissociations (private life, work, leisure, social and political life, "officialese" documents, and speech reduced to triviality and rhetoric). Social practice liberates itself spontaneously from whatever *institutes* separations, from the sum total of institutions. This is the meaning of the institutional crisis, which must not be reduced to a crisis of authority. Contestation does not arise against authority so much as against the entire society maintained by authority. Workers do not cease working because their employer acts like a father. They reject paternalism because it embodies and symbolizes a social order; their real target is the established social order.

Humiliation and boredom—the reverse side of authority, i.e. the power to make decisions—are as important as authority itself. On what does this authority weigh? It weighs on everyday existence—which it both institutes and constitutes as a condition. Under circumstances of tension and disorder, "uninterrupted speech," initiated and literally discovered in the event, challenged not only paternalist authority and the authority of the employers, but also the aim and finality of these authorities—the condition of everyday existence. It also challenged the repressive implications of this condition—a repressiveness which, through the use of common sense and trivial speech, sanctions triviality.

What is the purpose of so many reduced and therefore reductive activities? What is the objective which these activities make evident yet also dissimulate? To maintain a condition of everyday existence reduced to passive obedience. When the process of dis-alienation through unfettered speech, street activities, and spontaneous disorder—when this dis-alienation process ebbed, the order of everyday existence reorganized itself in its down-to-earth solidity. The disruptions of the social order come to be viewed as disruptions of everyday existence; the restoration of everyday existence supports the restoration of the social order. The suspension of everyday existence was defined in terms of the sum total of deprivations: no mail, no gasoline, no transportation, etc. The restoration of the availability of gasoline, postal service, railroads, money orders, and banking facilities involved the restoration not only of a few conveniences but also of something much more important—the totality of everyday existence. Together with a few use values, the reign of exchange-value and the world of the commodity were restored.

Everyday existence is a solid terrain which supports the structure because the structure was built on this terrain and made it hospitable to itself. The process—contestation, strike, the whole movement—shook up this terrain. This terrain is again solidifying, together with everything it carries and promotes: hierarchization, illusions, words. This does not mean that everyday existence can be transcended in one leap; it means that the dissociations which maintain everyday existence as the basic (down-to-earth) foundation of this society can be transcended in and by the process of self-management.

A careful and detailed study of the events may yet produce surprises. Beside the directives (imposed by specialized bodies), there were apparently also scattered and groping attempts at self-management. A beginning was made of the "thing" without the word, of action without thought. In several places the entire personnel, including the executive staff, usurped the functions of the foremen, occasionally even infringing on managerial functions. This means that the process has been initiated; but it is not irreversible.

Self-management indicates the road toward the transformation of everyday existence. "To change life"—this defines the meaning of the revolutionary process. But life is not changed magically by a poetic act, as the surrealists believed. Language liberated from its servitudes plays a necessary role —but it does not suffice. The transformation of everyday existence also involves institutions. In fact, it is not sufficient to speak, even less to write. The social practice capable of transcending dissociations and creating new institutions beyond those that affirm dissociations—this social practice has a name, but cannot be reduced to language.

11. The World Situation

Let us quickly review a few known aspects of the situation. Peaceful co-existence? It has its logic. The Soviet Union? It exists. The definition, Marxist or other, of socialism has little importance. From the viewpoint of absolute politics, the definition of socialism is an expression of ideology. The basic political fact? It is the existence of the U.S.S.R. and the strategy based on this existence. This does not favor the effort to establish a genuine socialist democracy in Western Europe. In the current conjuncture, such a new road might cause a number of countries to turn away from the Soviet Union: first of all Czechoslovakia, then other people's democracies (Poland, Hungary, Rumania), then other countries including Italy. Such a Europe linked with England would constitute a new political entity, which in turn would have an effect on state socialism. For reasons that are easy to understand, there are many who do not care for this prospect. State socialism remains the only official definition, criterion, program.

The United States? American imperialism? In 1945 their military presence on the European continent presumably made a revolutionary perspective impossible. Today they are busy elsewhere. It took a certain amount of bad faith to use the negotiations then beginning in Paris as an argument against the "agitators" and to accuse them of sabotage. American prestige moreover has fallen to its lowest level and the

"American way of life" no longer tempts anyone. The mythology and ideology of the United States have practically disappeared from the scene.

The last few years modified the image of history lived and absorbed by the youth. A strong intellectual current, in France and elsewhere, relegated history to the historical past for the benefit of an ideology—that of social organization through economic and technological rationality; but history continued. A classical view that has permeated Western culture holds that it is individuals who make history. A view of Marxist origin attributes this role to the masses. A view of world history that has emerged in recent times attributes the capacity for making history to minorities. The small Vietnamese nation is victoriously resisting the American giant. Fidel Castro and a few determined men have changed the face of a country and toppled a dictator. Che Guevara attempted to seize a continent. His figure has now assumed almost mythical proportions—it is he who made the "revolution in the revolution" a reality. The masses need ferment. The individuals who contribute to history-making accept a role which pledges them to heroism and sacrifice. Without their initiative and violence, nothing changes.

It is for specialists to examine the prospects of the Common Market and the gold question. The world situation has other aspects which political analysis must consider. Through an inverse shock wave, decolonization acts upon the industrialized countries, but in an unexpected manner. A country which oppresses other countries cannot be free. The ignorant or passive accomplices of oppression are themselves bound by the chains with which they bind the oppressed. How do colonizing countries regain their freedom? A paradoxical situation arises here. Regions, groups (the youth), sections of classes (workers or peasants) are becoming conscious of being colonized. By whom? By the centers of decision-making, power, and the accumulation of wealth—urban centers or rather centers constituted in the course of the explosion of the urban reality. Paradoxically, neo-capitalist exploitation has come to include internal colonization. This situation promotes increasing awareness. Organizational capitalism now has its colonies in the metropolis, and it concentrates on the internal market in order to utilize it according to a colonial pattern. The double exploitation of producer and consumer carries the colonial experience into the midst of the erstwhile colonizing people. This repercussion of the world situation on the national scene assumes various forms. The population in the metropolis is regrouped into ghettos (suburbs, foreigners, factories, students), and the new cities are to some extent reminiscent of colonial cities. The general oppression thus becomes characterized by complex differentiations which give new weight to democracy, unfettered speech, the exchange of ideas, and the discussion of projects—the only ways of undermining the isolation of the ghettos.

What is thus being contested is first of all an exploitation that is both strengthened and attenuated, but also know-how and power, and their junction in oppressive and repressive force. With the manifestation of differentiations (rightly stressed by Berque), there arises a social need for creation or "creativity." As this need arises, technology ceases to be felt as oppressive; the pervasiveness of technology itself helps undermine the fixed framework of know-how and power. This rebirth of differentiations and their manifestations accompanies both uneven development and the new contradictions which underlie it.

Consequently new cleavages arise. The oldest frontiers

between peoples and nations, established by the political action of the rising bourgeoisie, are in the process of disappearing. More recent but powerful psychological and physical boundaries between social classes, established at a time when industrial growth was dominant, are also disappearing. These boundaries have not yet been erased, but new and as yet scarcely visible limits are beginning to demarcate the centers of power (decision-making, wealth, and information) from their subordinate, semi-colonized dependencies. Around, by, and for these centers, the economic factor is transformed into political object, the object of political management. Hence the emergence of absolute politics—this illusion and phantom which unites the specters of power in the very midst of the void surrounding the exercise of power.

Revolutionary spontaneity is not unrelated to these recent cleavages that are now in the process of being effected in practice. It calls attention to them and demarcates them on a world-wide scale. Spontaneity attacks hierarchies because it aims at the poles of power. It cannot be explained merely by the material and functional conditions of proletarian life in industrial production. This type of explanation, although not yet irrelevant, will soon become obsolete. It is inadequate as an explanation of the international character of spontaneity, violence, contestation, and especially the international character of the student revolt. The ebullience and spontaneity in France may be due to the superposition of two kinds of social phenomena—those that can be understood in terms of old differentiations (social classes, positions, functions) in production, and those that can be understood only in terms of other factors (groups that are semi-colonized or view themselves as such, and are distributed as dependencies of the centers of power: ghettos, suburbs, outlying areas, the youth, students). Any other explanation remains confined to a partial psychological or psychoanalytical viewpoint (see especially the articles of Edgar Morin in *Le Monde,* June 5-6, 1968). Such a reductive and reduced perspective is not political.

It is certainly inexact to say that the era of non-abundance has disappeared on a world scale. The advanced (industrialized, urbanized) countries, however, have overcome scarcity. It is certain that new organizational forms superseding the institutions which are historically linked to non-abundance, and whose function it is to distribute an inadequate social surplus, are coming to the fore. This phenomenon, which is taking place on a world scale, gives rise to new plans, interpretations, and projects.

12. Urban Phenomena

The analysis now turns to a problem which is itself important in the overall complex of problems. Since there are new phenomena—especially the problems connected with the urbanization of industrial society—how should we define the links that exist between these groups of phenomena? Should we speak of juxtaposition, superposition, "overdetermination"? Analysis must reject metaphors, and especially mechanistic analogies (detonator, resonance, etc.). These describe but also displace the problem. These metaphors tend to separate *cause* (the student movement) and *effect* (the general strike, the institutional crisis), by stressing the disproportion between cause and effect. Such an approach is doubly unsound: it is theoretically wrong and it depreciates the movement. If they had struck down only the capitalism of know-how and capitalist know-how, the bourgeoisie of knowledge as opposed to knowledge of the bourgeoisie, the students could not be regarded as the immediate cause of vaster phenomena. The analytic approach used until now leads to a conclusion which opens up new analytic possibilities. The process under consideration implies two distinct series of reasons and causes—those that deal with the analysis of (old and new) contradictions, and those that deal with the analysis of uneven development (which dissimulates, aggravates or alternates the contradictions).

On the social and political level, *the centers of production* have not altogether lost their importance. Far from it. Self-management and the process initiated by it must start out from these centers to be able to permeate the entire society. But *the centers of decision-making*—know-how and power, information, and accumulation of wealth and technology—are increasingly arousing interest and assuming importance. This is a peculiarly urban phenomenon, or an aggregate of urban phenomena. A two-fold effect may be anticipated. These phenomena lead to new contradictions. In relation to the new phenomena, moreover, the old (ideological and institutional) superstructures—rooted in the period of industrialization, and its social and political relations—may become subject to lags—growing or diminishing, open or hidden. This also applies to political superstructures, the specialized and institutionalized machinery.

The separations and dissociations have their cause and reasons in the technological and social division of labor. The technological division must be understood as operative in terms of the level and organization of the productive forces. The social division—which includes the bureaucratic hierarchies—is superposed on the technological division, aggravates its effects and modifies it in keeping with the interests and rationality of capitalist management. This technological and social division of labor must therefore be viewed in terms of the "imperatives" of production and industrial growth. It is eventually projected onto open terrain. The effects and implications of segregation—an extreme form of the division of labor in terms of which it is localized and organized—are also added to previous dissociations. They maintain and aggravate these dissociations by situating them in fixed social areas. Functions that could previously be separated only through social analysis, now become separated through action. Formerly abstract and incomplete, the dissociations now become complete. Projected onto the terrain, it is here that they can transcend themselves—in the streets. It is here that student meets worker, and reason reduced to a function again recovers speech. Ideologies—particularly that of pure analytic intellect—are realized in practice. Institutions rule. And thus it is that these ideologies and institutions come to lag behind, bogged down as they are in their very achievements. Urban phenomena accompany the withering of the superstructure of industrial growth (including "urbanism"). This growth, which proved incapable of promoting social development, becomes discredited, together with its ideology, rationality, and institutions.

The new proletariat? The "new working class"? They do not meet in the highly technological industries, but in middle-income housing projects, and new towns and neighborhoods. This proletariat no longer experiences former wants or the old scars of the proletarian condition. It is housed, fed, entertained. Economists may view this "standard of living" as satisfactory. It satisfies no one—whether in terms of individual needs, or so-called social and cultural needs, or way of life. The working class submits reluctantly to this condition of need and non-participation. Humiliation and the lack of freedom resulting from the presence (and absence) of the centers of decision-making and social life are keenly felt. The many forms of alienation are experienced obscurely, and provoke muffled and profound anxiety. This is the source of the surge of spontaneity. Working class youths grow up with hatred—blind or conscious—for the pressures exerted by authority, and for the whole range of established "realities." The previous generation voiced mainly economic demands. It demanded and still demands consumer goods, wage increases, an end to traditional poverty; but the new generation demands something else. It is no longer seduced, satisfied, or overwhelmed by refrigerators and automobiles.

This youth seeks and perhaps initiates a new way of life. These young people have finished with an insipid *"yé-yé"* romanticism; they have gone beyond it and are now making their way toward a revolutionary romanticism, without theory yet highly effective. They have surprising ways of expressing their demands—they demand while contesting and contest while demanding. Those who have seen them at demonstrations were surprised at their style: relaxed amid violence, setting off for the conquest of city and life with a transcendent audacity, and frequently carrying the black flag.

This is surely a new working-class generation, but there is no conflict between the generations. This youth was sensitized and fashioned by the conditions under which it grew up. These conditions are not peculiar to them alone. These young people bear witness to a situation shared by all ages.

Under these conditions, a new sense of the world and history was dimly yet powerfully absorbed. Contestation feeds on it. There is a generation gap but nothing approaching a struggle between generations. Such a view *reduces* political phenomena to psycho-sociological attitudes.

As for self-management, it cannot confine itself to the centers of production. The ongoing process extends to all areas of society—wherever there are "users." The network of "base" organizations must cover all "interests"—or it will continue to shrink. The Yugoslav model shows the necessary extension of self-management to the "users" of urban reality, to the entire reality viewed under the two-fold aspect of production and consumption, exchange and use. It also reveals the difficulties involved. The Chinese model of commune—in spite of vast differences—exhibits the same orientation. In this perspective, numerous urban realities that arose or were revealed in recent times take on a new meaning which analysis is gradually uncovering. Knowledge of urban phenomena is as yet in its beginnings; so is the urban practice itself, which is slowly becoming divorced from industrial praxis.

13. "Mutation"

Events lend themselves to various analyses and versions. Dogmatism has always been incompatible with a scientifiic approach. Viewpoints and perspectives are not subject to uniform rules. The convergence or divergence of these relative and limited viewpoints, however, must be shown. This question can be posed and resolved only on the level of praxis, i.e. the political level.

An event may be examined in terms of *knowledge* or content. This content may be viewed as analytic or synthetic, partial or all-inclusive, it may be divided into "disciplines" or unified by an overall conception. The event may be viewed also in terms of its transmission—i.e. its pedagogic form, which may be more or less authoritarian and dogmatic, and more or less determined by the content or purpose of an institution and its social function. This in turn results in a critical analysis of institutions, among which events have thrown the spotlight on the university. In terms of analysis, the relations between institution and society thus come to the fore. Such an analysis makes it possible to study functions and dysfunctions and institutional results, and involves institutions as well as society viewed in its totality. The analysis focuses alternately on institutions and society in a reciprocal critique.

One particularly important analysis has been advanced on several occasions. Starting from the technological division of (social) labor, it stresses the social division of labor which, superposed on the technological division, modifies and "overdetermines" it. How do hierarchization and bureaucratization manipulate technological imperatives and necessities so as to transform them into a social scale of prestige, power, and revenue? Instead of merely ascertaining and affirming such a scale in the name of empiricism, or emphasizing its importance in the name of operationalism, critical knowledge on the contrary would participate in contestation and strengthen it. Is this kind of analysis possible? Events have shown that a (contesting) practice which upsets established separations and hierarchizations opens the way for analysis. It shatters the apologetic ideologies which have made it difficult and perhaps impossible to examine extremely complex interactions.

An analysis of this kind could proceed from a fresh conception of ideology. The "classical" Marxist view of social classes and their relations—the middle classes and their fluctuations, the working class and its economic and political problems—is still important. But only if analysis frees itself from the dogmatism and authoritarianism characteristic of political apparatuses. It has long been intolerable that the capacity for decision-making of central structures should weigh upon analysis, and suppress and paralyze dialectical reason and the critical power of its rationality (which in essence "is" movement, is linked to movement, and captures conjuncture and the event).

France is the land where, more than anywhere else, the historical class struggles were each time fought out to a decision, and where, consequently, the changing political forms within which they move and in which their results are summarized have been stamped in the sharpest outlines. The centre of feudalism in the Middle Ages, the model country of unified monarchy, resting on estates, since the Renaissance, France demolished feudalism in the Great Revolution and established the unalloyed rule of the bourgeoisie in a classical purity unequalled by any other European land. And the struggle of the upward-striving proletariat against the ruling bourgeoisie appeared here in an acute form unknown elsewhere. This was the reason why Marx not only studied the past history of France with particular predilection, but also followed her current history in every detail, stored up the material for future use and, consequently, events never took him by surprise. (Friedrich Engels, Preface to the third German edition, 1885, of *The Eighteenth Brumaire of Louis Bonaparte*, New York, 1963, pp. 13-14.)

Proletarian revolutions . . . criticize themselves constantly, interrupt themselves continually in their own course, come back to the apparently accomplished in order to begin it afresh, deride with unmerciful thoroughness the inadequacies, weaknesses and paltrinesses of their first attempts, seem to throw down their adversary only in order that he may draw new strength from the earth and rise again, more gigantic, before them, recoil ever and anon from the indefinite prodigiousness of their own aims, until a situation has been created which makes all turning back impossible, and the conditions themselves cry out: Hic Rhodus, hic salta! (Karl Marx, *The Eighteenth Brumaire*, p. 19.)

What matters is not to propose a theory of the movement, but to show the movement in its true character and elaborate the elements of a theory. There is a movement; there are therefore theoretical needs and requirements. A theory of the movement has to emerge from the movement itself, for it is the movement that has revealed, unleashed, and liberated theoretical capacities. No contribution to the elaboration of such a theory can lay claim to being an established doctrine; it can never be more than a limited contribution.

Viewed in terms of the analysis of urban phenomena, the movement unfolded in several stages; it moved from one social arena to another. Originating in the Faculty of Letters (and Humanities) of Nanterre, it spread to Paris and then to the provinces. The Latin Quarter and the venerable Sorbonne became its focus.

Let us review the sequence and interconnection of events.

Nanterre

This is a Parisian Faculty located outside of Paris. It is not far from the area of *La Defense* (commercial buildings, truck depots). It may become an urban center by 1980. Right now it contains misery, shantytowns, excavations for an express subway line, low-income housing projects for workers, industrial enterprises. This is a desolate and strange landscape. The Faculty was conceived in terms of the concepts of the industrial production and productivity of neo-capitalist society, but falls short of the implications of such a conception. The buildings and the environment reflect the real nature of the intended project. It is an enterprise designed to produce mediocre intellectuals and "junior executives" for the management of this society, and transmit a body of specialized knowledge determined and limited by the social division of labor. It had from the beginning a well-defined function—topically and typically—which was to reveal itself slowly in its day-to-day activities, but very rapidly once the movement began. Situated in the midst of a civilization which, from the City of antiquity to the historic city of the European West, is based on the City, it might be described as a place of damnation.

The suburbs and their shantytowns are more than a sad spectacle—they constitute a void. *Anomie* and "social marginality" are an integral part of the image projected by this society. Absence is "where unhappiness becomes concrete." This specimen of wall-writing says exactly what it means. In these surroundings work loses all meaning. In the Faculty—a product of industrialization and de-urbanization —the absence of civilization is transformed into obsession. Education can hardly be expected to fill this void, especially in view of the fact that the content and form of knowledge lag behind the intended project. The City—past, absent, future—assumes a *utopian* value for the boys and girls caught up in a *heterotopia* which generates tensions and obsessive fantasies.

Nanterre is marked by a two-fold segregation—functional and social, and industrial and urban. Functionalized by initial design, culture was transported to a ghetto of students and teachers situated in the midst of other ghettos filled with the "abandoned," subject to the compulsions of production, and driven into an extra-urban existence. An absurd "urbanistic" frame of mind—the ideology that goes by the name of "urbanism"—planned these functional buildings that are utterly devoid of character.

On the social level, extreme forms of segregation have paradoxical effects. The university community in which the "function of living" becomes specialized and reduced to a bare minimum (the habitat)—while traditional separations between boys and girls, and between work and leisure and privacy, are maintained—this community becomes the focus of sexual aspirations and rebellions. The slightest prohibition or regulation becomes intolerable. It is rejected not because of its effects—which are usually quite negligible—but because it *symbolizes* repression. Official or officious liberalism in this connection revals its own limitations, and this always surprises liberals: "They are allowed to do this and that, almost everything. After all, a minimum of order is necessary. We cannot permit chaos." The power of symbols is lost on liberal ideology—it avows its own impotence or turns into authoritarianism.

The Faculty buildings were designed for the functions of education: vast amphitheaters, small "functional" rooms, drab halls, an administrative wing—the meaning of this morphology will soon become apparent. All this becomes the focus of political rebellion. In such an environment the "ordinary" begins to assume surprising "extraordinary" qualities—an everyday life permeated by culture, with manifest poverty sharply contrasting with the utopian and mythical richness of officially proposed culture and officially dispensed specialized knowledge. It is here that—more intensely than elsewhere—life partakes both of reality (its misery) and imagination (the splendor of history and the world!). This contributes substantially to the disintegration of culture, formal knowledge, and institutions.

Segregation is an experience as well as a physical environment, and its effects may operate inversely. What happens to the boys and girls from the well-to-do neighborhoods of Paris and the western suburbs? Many—the best—experience a malaise approaching acute anxiety. Having witnessed the spectacle of misery, they move beyond spectacle. Mixing of classes? Fusion? Not quite. Interaction would be a better word. It is quite natural for students of bourgeois origin to turn against their native "milieu." The phenomenon is by no means new, except perhaps in terms of the number involved and the quality of their revolt. It is possible to give a psycho-sociological or even psychoanalytical explanation of this attitude. These young people disapprove equally of traditional domination by the father, professorial and political paternalism, and employers. They continue, on a higher level, the revolt against the Fathers, the conflict between the generations. It is in the name of this revolt that they adopt a radical negativity which begins, inevitably, on the verbal level. Verbal violence leads to violent action.

Such a psychoanalytic or psycho-sociological explanation, however, is inadequate. It explains to some extent the attitude, but not its political content. Let us repeat: the crisis of authority is but the outward appearance of a much deeper crisis which extends, beyond everyday existence, to the institutions and the state which holds them together. The psychological explanation fails to take into account the practical and theoretical experience of these students; they are generally widely read beyond the requirements of their courses. Many of the students of modest means have very positive preoccupations—courses, examinations, employment. At the outset of their student life some do not consider themselves sufficiently secure to engage in political activity, or even to do any outside reading. They are troubled by what they see. What does this society hold in store for them? Sometimes these same students demand a job while rejecting society as thoroughly as the others; but they do so by different means. The politicization of the others is more concrete. In their experience of a society which offers them no security, adventure, assurances, or seductions, they are aware only of the absence of possibilities. The prospect of holding a "junior" position in education, industry, or the bureaucratic hierarchy, worry over slow promotion, bills, transfers, apartments, and cars—this image of everyday existence is far from appealing.

Those who are not pressed by immediate, concrete worries,

search for more inspiring motivations; those who are overcome by the pressures of reality, withdraw. This situation results in a coalition of all these currents—which go beyond the traditional class distinctions (bourgeoisie, middle class and petty bourgeoisie, proletariat)—against a common enemy. An original dialectic movement begins to emerge—social marginality against centralization, *anomie* against norms, contestation against decisions. These apparently privileged students—"public opinion" is aware of little else but these "privileges"—begin to take their places in the forefront of the political struggle. They become part of the vanguard.

Under these circumstances, the continued functioning of institutions will inevitably accentuate their—to use sociological jargon—dysfunctions. All attempts to reabsorb these dysfunctions will fail. The emergence of anomic groups—the famous *groupuscules*—becomes inevitable. They derive from different critical reactions to contemporary history, in terms of Marxism-Leninism, Trotskyism, the struggles of Fidel Castro or Che Guevara. These *groupuscules* cause a ferment, a leavening; they challenge everything including themselves and one another. This is the source of the movement which swept them all along and which, under their impact, is incessantly transformed by discussion. The movement embraced all these groups without dissolving or absorbing them. Though composed of many groups, it was and remains more than the sum total of these groups. Each group may have been autonomous; in the movement, each group grew and contributed to the growth of the whole. This original phenomenon derives from the unfettered speech that characterized all the confrontations, and therefore from the absence of dogma and pre-established rules.

Is this a pathogenic milieu, what might be called an artificial culture? No, this is a malicious interpretation. Such a movement is perfectly normal if its premises are granted: freedom of speech, politicization in depth (radical contestation is counterposed to the absolute politics of the government), creation of a new type of leadership. Far from being pathological, such a conjunction even assumes a cathartic function. Freedom of speech sustains equilibrium and strength. The Faculty—whose intended function it is to transmit a type of knowledge that fulfills neither promises nor needs—becomes a "social condenser" and the focus of a whole range of prevalent questions and problems. The Faculty has become such a focus, not for reasons of architecture or urbanism, but, on the contrary, because it is a negatively privileged place. This fragment of a broken, rejected, and marginal university regains a kind of universality. Among the students *all* tendencies manifest themselves, especially *all* those which oppose the established society. Even the institution called university, which has in fact already exploded, and which thought that it could regain strength and autonomy in a marginal location, is dissolving. The crack, the outlet for tensions and latent pressures, is widening.

What does this mean? It indicates a failure of the cultural enterprise—i.e. the failure of the transmission of a type of knowledge conceived in terms of industrial enterprises and designed to serve the interests of these enterprises. Even though the needs of the market, material production, and the division of labor did not completely dominate the curriculum —here there is a lag—architectural and urbanist morphology is in advance of the content and form of the curriculum and has rendered it impotent. But this morphology itself already lagged behind the requirements of social life and "culture."

This superposition of reasons and causes has resulted in significant failure. The degree of lag and imbalance (between education and project, between project and the possibilities and needs of social practice) masks and dissimulates contradictions which manifest themselves—in the movement!

The famous escalation—all too often represented as an escalation of violence alone—can be analyzed:

From the point of view of the "subject."

These initial groups—elements of the forces that are mobilized around and within them—are an integral part of the movement. The rising wave flows across or around the obstacles, submerges the dams and all attempts to recuperate, neutralize, and channel it. Between deviations toward university legality (opportunities for "free discussion") and pure and simple brutality (riots), the movement continues to widen. It does not involve large numbers of people attached to norms; and it stands for active democracy rather than the rules of formal democracy. What stages of development does this entail? It moves from critical thought to demands, from demands to contestation, from theoretical contestation to contesting practice. With this last stage, the subjective factor assumes a different quality and meaning—it is transformed into objective intervention.

From the point of view of the object and "objectives."

The movement at first concentrated on specifically economic objectives: buildings, credits, employment, market restraints, imperatives of the division of labor. These old demands—inadequately but forcefully taken over by the bureaucratic trade-union and political apparatus—were soon superseded.

The movement began to raise questions of ideology and "values." The question of specialized knowledge came to the fore. This type of knowledge—fragmented, departmentalized —is condemned by the most perceptive students. Ideology closes the gaps resulting from fragmentation by giving it the appearance of totality. Inclusive knowledge of the world, history, and human and social reality, always promised but never provided—these disappointing crumbs make it impossible to accept the ideology in which they are enveloped. There is no criterion for distinguishing ideology from specialized knowledge, and suspect interpretations from the various disciplines. In addition, the students violently attack the form of education, which they accuse of masking the deficiencies of content by high-handedly imposing both ideology and fragmented knowledge.

At this stage the slogan of a "critical university" becomes all-important. The students hesitate between two approaches: a parallel university devoted to the critique of the official university, and a permanent critique within the official university. But they accept neither the project of a critical university, nor that of an autonomous university (or department), whether in the guise of co-management or self-management. They initiate a great contestation of the entire society, its institutions, its ideologies. They face, effectively and practically, the problems of state, information, police, power. From this point on, the faculties can no longer remain the focus of such objectives.

Before discussing the movement as it unfolded within the capital—"the movement" here does not refer to any particular group, but to its overall dynamic character—a misunderstanding must be cleared up. It is incorrect to say that the movement became gradually political, that it moved from a non-political to a political stage. The movement was profoundly political from the outset; this is one of its most forcefully original characteristics. The elements which initiated it—*groupuscules* or other—in fact rejected any abstract thinking rooted in an ideological and institutional separation of intellectual and political life. Whatever their political coloration—revolutionary, Trotskyist, Maoist, etc.—they had bridged the gap between thought and practice. Does this imply the "theory of the spark" that ignites an inflammable situation? Not quite. What proved fateful was not any particular mode of thought. The movement was made possible by the initial act of a mode of thought that rejected previously established conditions. In spite of all divergences, this was a collective act. The "theory of the spark" has been vulgarized, giving rise to various metaphors, including that of a "detonator," which has been officially advanced. The political effectiveness of an active minority (or active minorities) cannot be understood in terms of such crude descriptions or arguments which assume that analytical problems—especially that of juncture—have already been solved. What happened when the student movement began to penetrate the working class? How did the workers view this movement before joining it, when they were about to intensify it? What was the role of the working-class youth?

It is absurd to attack the student movement after the fact and maintain that it was but an insignificant agitation and that a few tanks and machine guns would have prevented this attempt at urban guerrilla warfare. This may be true, but it does not answer the question. The extraordinary fact is that, following a relatively minor confrontation, a substantial number of the superstructures and institutions of a great country should have been severely shaken and in certain cases even made to collapse. For such were the results of the movement as it spread.

To understand what happened, certain categories and concepts must be changed or rejected. This movement is *unthinkable* in terms of the mental categories of specialized politics. But the movement existed. Actual or potential, it still exists. The question is not to deny its existence, but to think it through. The question, for a whole category of people who think in terms of certain concepts and who possess power, is *to think the unthinkable.*

The movement was almost "pure," almost entirely movement. It was the contrary of a state—it was a continuous act, continuously new or renewed. It was almost devoid of "subject" and "object"—i.e. it transcended the mental categories of object and subject, and revealed them as inadequate. The movement had very little support. It was a paradoxical stage of political consciousness. It is precisely this that cannot be understood in terms of the mental structures associated with political structures. There is a search for answers, and an attempt to find, at any cost, meaning in terms of the traditional categories of object and subject. This leads to talk of plots, conspiracics, infernal machines. Some explain the movement in terms of a crisis of leadership, others view it as a conflict between opposing sides. But what is really involved is action and an activist movement endowed with intense, rapid, and lucid perception of immediate possibilities. Such a movement is the paradoxical answer of political spontaneity to absolute politics and cannot fail to grow. If its growth is halted, it must collapse, even if its repercussions widen in other respects.

This is an almost "pure" movement, but it contains internal

contradictions. These contradictions give it a powerful impulsion, animate it, and endow it with mobility. As soon as it collapses, the hidden contradictions which it seemingly had overcome are liberated. Nothing now remains visible except its blemishes. The elements that gave the movement strength are forgotten. As the events fade, they come to be viewed as "pure" events which vanish without leaving traces, and which do not conform to predictions and interpretations or to the movement of history—they seem "pure" evanescence. It is quite true that the (capitalist) mode of production has not disappeared, that its "base" still exists, that old and unresolved problems are appearing again, and that the accumulation of specialized knowledge remains intact. It is now easy to maintain that the movement was marked by pathos, inflated language, lack of will, lack of overall projects and theory—all the weaknesses of a movement which, in a given conjuncture, appeared as the only organized force capable of crystallizing a wide range of aspirations. Common sense now exclaims: "The time was not ripe for action!" The cold and static analysis of effervescence, contagious solidarity, and mobility becomes false and unfair. It is nothing more than an approach based on obsolete categories. The causes of (relative) failure become evident after failure has become evident. It is forgotten that it is the limitations of spontaneity that are involved—a necessary spontaneity rather than failure.

The situation results in a dissociation that is more serious than all the dissociations and separations which spontaneity tried to overcome. A new, extremely profound contradiction has taken root in the revolutionary movement, in France and throughout the world. On one side—institutionalized revolution with its apparatus, doctrine, rationality, mental and social categories, basic immobility; on the other side—a spontaneity that is rejected and refuted as irrational and unthinkable, therefore impossible, and explainable only in terms characteristic of the police mind. This is a circle, a merry-go-round. One side stimulates the other, which in turn escapes and disavows it. Is "awareness" of this situation of any consequence? Perhaps. But there is a profound break in this vicious circle. The end has not yet come. The minorities have together rejected everything that made thought ineffective, social life inert, and political life poverty-stricken. Hence their unexpected strength. The new, initial and basic element of the movement thus manifests itself. The explosive strength and impact of the movement derives from the state of French society and the movement itself, and the relations between them.

The movement was able to unleash a cultural revolution only by not being "cultural," by not being fixated in ideology or culture. It struck at culture, but only by aiming and striking at politics. It spontaneously situated itself at the juncture. This movement may be described, sociologically, as constituting a "subject," a "collective subject," a "historical subject." This is not false. But it does not define its political essence as expressed by its spokesmen, who still have to give it a theoretical formulation. The striking characteristic of the movement is that it was able to hold its own without apparatus or institution, that it had an organization without fixed structure, and that it took politically intelligent decisions without a pre-established program and "leaders" (there were only spokesmen). These are highly original characteristics.

During the weeks when the movement was in constant motion, the void of the university became filled with effervescence. The administration and the majority of the faculty members, of course, viewed this as disorder, threat, absurd agitation. The reactionary frame of mind again had recourse to its Manichean mythology—evil against good, disorder against order, barbarism against culture. Relatively insignificant material or moral facts were erected into symbols of evil, juvenile barbarism, adolescent savagery. But certain creative tendencies also came to light. Widespread discussion of the "consumer society" produced photographic collages and montages, magazine articles, and certain quotations and slogans, that deserved better than immediate condemnation. The authorities did not welcome the birth of a spontaneous mural art. In the midst of the effervescence that filled places long marked by emptiness, there was a sparkling animation—celebration, humor, elements of playfulness (always directly related to action and political life)—blended with demands and aspirations, crystallizing them and channeling them against a repressive environment. At this point, discourse became marked by an impertinent and significant opposition. "Transgression" was opposed to folklore. Whatever could not be characterized as transgression, immediately became folklore. The leaders are transgressing; those who will not follow them become part of the realm of folklore. Horrified and impotent, the adherents of norms witness the sequence of transgressions. They are unable to conceive of the initial transgression: the crossing of the border that "normally" separates the political and non-political areas, and the ensuing emancipation. They cannot understand that absolute politicization—marked by the separation of the political and non-political areas, and using this dissociation to maintain both itself and control over the whole of social life—must eventually have repercussions at the "base." The elementary and spontaneous "base" becomes aware of the fact that it is political, and that "culture" is political—i.e. ideological.

The authorities function in keeping with their norms and policies, which they view as administrative rather than political. This is also the manner of all bureaucratic categories, including the liberal bureaucracy. The movement did not become politicized as a result of any "mistakes," or the arrival of the Nanterre students in the Latin Quarter. From that day on, however, the movement began to spread to new ground. Formed elsewhere, it now found itself in new, extremely favorable conditions, but also engaged in increasingly bitter struggles. The movement oscillated between urban celebration and violence, between playfulness and urban guerrilla warfare; it had all these different and complementary aspects. The expression "urban guerrillas," used by the officials, fits those who are officially called "the forces of order" better than it does the students. The student guerrillas, in spite of their courage, cannot achieve a strategic level; the police, however, can—they have the means. There was among the students a very meaningful fluctuation between playfulness and a violence which orients celebration toward tragedy. The Paris Commune provides an outstanding example of such a dramatic orientation. Edgar Morin has referred to a student Commune. More brilliant than correct, this formulation overlooks decisive differences. In 1871 the people was armed. The entire people took to the streets and engaged in celebration and struggle. The bourgeoisie had already left the capital or was preparing to do so. It was not therefore a marginal category of "citizens" that intervened in the situation by abolishing separations. One analogy can be made. In March 1871 as in May 1968, people who had come from the outlying areas into which they had been driven and where they had found nothing but a social void assembled and proceeded together toward the reconquest of the urban centers.

Celebration and struggle—this ambiguity characterizes certain urban phenomena. It is a condensation and intensification of what has happened in the villages over the centuries. Let us first look at celebration—laughter, unfettered speech, humor, song. During the demonstrations, Paris changed and was restored—the vistas, the streets, the Boulevard Saint-Michel which, rid of automobiles, again became a promenade and forum. Trangression and creation go together (witness the white and blood-covered Nō masks surrounding a mannequin hung from the gallows during the demonstration of Monday, May 13, as well as innumerable signs and inscriptions). Transgression, without prior project, pursues its work. It leaps over boundaries, liberates, wipes out limits, introduces new cleavages.

A dialectical interaction between marginality and urban centrality was at the same time initiated. Action came to center in the Sorbonne. A center had become necessary, and it could not be found within the "heterotopia" of Nanterre. The movement originated in this outlying area, but abandoned it temporarily. The students reoccupied the Latin Quarter; they re-appropriated the space that had been taken from them and reconquered it in sharp struggle. Action invested the Latin Quarter with new meaning; its inner meaning reappeared, amplified and intensified. As a result, the old Sorbonne hung with red and black flags took on a transfigured and symbolic dimension. It was no longer an abstraction representing a remote culture and "scientificity." A concrete utopia now proclaimed a unified culture transcending the division of labor and fragmented specializations. The fetishism of specialization disintegrated.

Viewed in its emphatic sense, the *utopian* locality came to assume an extraordinary presence. This culture, with the hope it inspires, is no longer the classical, pre-capitalist, pre-industrial culture that survives in liberal humanism and obsolete Encyclopedism; nor is it the ideology of capitalist and neo-capitalist society—a dissolving and disintegrating ideology that meets the requirements of the market and the social division of labor (by promoting fragmented intellectual skills). A new culture is in the making. While awaiting its fulfillment and in order to create it, a kind of explosion shook the Sorbonne, which again became central and relevant. This was the explosion of unfettered speech. It took a devastating revenge on the constraints of written language. Speech manifested itself as a primary freedom, now re-conquered and re-appropriated. Speech, repressed during the repressive and terrorist period, burst forth in the crowded lecture halls, courtyard, on the square, in the vast forum. Who took the floor? All those present—both students and people who had never crossed (and sometimes had never before dared cross) the portals of this sanctuary consecrated to private knowledge, mysterious writings, and class-permeated scientificity. One had but to listen to discover what people had on their minds during the period when esoteric writing held sway—the best and the worst, unanswerable questions, profound or absurd arguments, apparent or real boldness, good and bad conscience. In this verbal delirium, there unfolded a vast psychodrama, or rather a vast social therapy, an ideological cure for intellectuals and non-intellectuals, who finally met. All this speech had to be expressed for the event to exist and leave traces.

What must be emphasized—and cannot as yet be grasped clearly because it was inconceivable a few weeks earlier—is the sudden extension of the movement. Marginal at first, then finding or creating a center, it leaped forward and reached the outlying areas. It is difficult in this remarkable outburst to demarcate the effects of cultural symbolism, indignation with an order maintained by force, exemplary action ending the separations of social life. Through dramatic, violent, and precipitous episodes the movement began to permeate the entire society. Instead of avoiding a confrontation with the state, the cultural revolution threatened it. Ideologies and words, institutions with their assumptions and "values"—the whole range of superstructures began to falter. It was as though many people suddenly realized that they no longer believed in their activities—this applies to artists, actors, newscasters, teachers, production workers. The newscasters were tired of being ordered to lie, the actors of entertaining and pleasing people condemned to boredom. The entire system of alibis, false emphases, and social reflections could be said to be disappearing because it was exposed in a central point.

Through localized or generalized phenomena (strikes, occupations, demonstrations) and through the relations of generations, groups, and classes, something new and different was emerging. To use a metaphor, it appeared as though the entire society swayed and masked by the state assumed the material state which physicists call "metastable." This is but a metaphor. False equilibrium, false coherence, illusory coherence—society carries with it all these dense, heterogeneous elements, these survivals, these parasitic accretions and superfluities. Under the sway of the state and absolute politics, society constitutes a distorted system. Its systematic appearance derives from an ideology and an illusion. It is not the system that is disintegrating—it is the illusion of a system and the illusion of a coherent rationality that are being dissipated. Motivations, to use a current expression, images and fantasies—in brief, ideologies and incentives—begin to lose their force. The cultural revolution and the political revolution blend; this is the result of activities transcending the dissociation of the cultural and political areas. Bureaucratic machines rooted in an economic base remain intact. They are the only remaining supports of the social relations which created them and which they cannot change without destroying themselves or which they will not change. They play an unexpected role. They become the solid poles or axes around which an order that was shaken from top to bottom reconstitutes itself.

These pillars of order held their own; but they did so with the help of operations that were more or less conscious, and difficult to analyze because they were new or rather newly revealed. An interplay of substitutions and "representations" takes place. The organized working class—i.e. the trade unions—are substituted for the working class. The trade unions are replaced with a trade-union apparatus that is distinct from the political apparatus; these trade-union bureaucratic machines proclaim this difference (on the ideological and institutional levels), but they are nevertheless political instruments. In the very act of asserting its strength, the most "representative" trade-union bureaucracy reveals the weakness, and the social and political isolation, of the working class. In hailing the working class, it confirms this isolation. It emphasizes the weakness of the working class at the very moment when the working class shows its strength, overcomes its isolation and proves itself capable of assuming power. It is a strange logic of the situation, which is absorbed into the (institutional and ideological) logic of society at the very moment this logic is exploding.

The fact remains that historians will have to study this remarkable situation. For several hours social disintegration assumed extreme proportions. This was not due primarily to the fact that the tidal wave submerged everything, including the innermost centers of the regime. It was due rather to the fact that the void surrounding these centers—or whatever remained of them—widened, and isolated them. Consequently, everything that was supposed to "function" ceased to function. The departments charged with the maintenance of order were isolated, and the command posts reduced to impotence. Panic and insubordination broke out in high places. Power was not vacated; the regime and its representatives were actively present. It is the entire society that became vacant; and there was no one to occupy it. Those who could have done so were governed by ideological and institutional attitudes that prevented them from acting in this direction. History became silent, and even dual power did not exist.

After reaching the crest of the wave, the movement began to ebb. Its impressive growth masked its decline. The widespread occupation of the centers of production and the powerful but partial demands lead us to forget that the centers of power and decision-making resumed their functions. Historically, this was a retreat. The movement, however, continued. Its quantitative extension toward the outlying areas was not sufficient to define it. Although efforts were being made to limit and reduce it, it had qualitative implications. It continued to transgress the limitations that were being imposed. It tried in particular to free itself from an old dilemma—either all-embracing, total revolution, or fragmented activities that must inevitably degenerate into reformism.

With admirable and spontaneous boldness, the movement tried consciously to unite cultural and political revolution, workers and students. It began to elaborate a project of generalized self-management and, in this sense, engaged in *social practice.* Activist strikers went so far as to attempt the formation of a kind of economy parallel to the neocapitalist economy (direct links between producers and consumers, and in certain regions between peasants and workers). There were plans to force the state to abandon its control over key sectors, especially national education and pedagogic and ideological training. The project of generalized self-management extended to all levels of society (material and intellectual production, services, urban life). This social practice, as we have stressed earlier, tried to express itself almost everywhere. The interaction of center and periphery revealed the importance of a new social, political, and cultural sphere—*urban society* which brings with it a new set of problems. The centrality achieved and maintained by the movement sent this movement back to the margins of urban reality—to the suburbs, outlying areas, production and housing centers. The movement reverberated from these margins back toward the centers of decision-making. But it did so without occupying these centers. The demonstrations against the Bourse were an attack against a symbol situated in the center of the city and symbolic representation, yet outside the centers in which real decisions are made.

The anticipated urban society is becoming a reality on the material and social "base" of an urban life that has been restored and transformed. The segregations and multiple dissociations which had been projected onto the terrain in the explosion of the city, are now transcended. Seen in this light, the events take on a different meaning. In the uneven development of society, above the old and new contradictions, three layers of interacting superstructures (institutions and ideologies) are superimposed:

a. Superstructures dating from a pre-capitalist and pre-industrial period, when agricultural production and peasant life, with its image and representation of the world, still predominated.

b. Superstructures dating from the period of industrialization and situated within a social framework established by the bourgeoisie, capitalism, and private ownership of the means of production (but it must not be forgotten that the technological base of industrialization continues to change: automation, information storage).

c. As yet ill-defined superstructures emerging from the transformation of society within an obsolescent framework (the framework of consumer society, organizational capitalism or monopoly capital linked to the state). This transformation in depth can be defined as an emergent *urban society*, with its own problems and requirements.

The effect of shock, or rather rupture, which the events produced on the superstructures took place when distortions accumulated and hidden contradictions revealed themselves. The breaking point: the university, culture. The point of departure: the areas marked by de-urbanization, segregation and, therefore, by an inverse impulse to overcome the dissociations. Strong points achieved by the movement: its reconquest or achievement of centrality in the face of the established centers of decision-making (bureaucratic machines and specific topology), which remained solid in spite of the upheaval.

An important and authoritarian segment of this society continues to defend a crumbling, disintegrating, and obsolete culture which this segment uses for repressive purposes. Another "modern" segment aims at fairly rapid, skillfully engineered adjustments. As for the rising forces, they aim at a transformed culture that is no longer outside of life, but conveys or "expresses" a way of life. This culture will no longer be a culture in the old sense of the term. But it cannot unfold in the abstract. It requires more than mental space. It requires a space that is both symbolic and material, an appropriated or re-appropriated morphology. Primarily u-topian, a unitary culture established on a higher level and on a new technological and socio-economic base requires space and time; but these must become different. The specifically utopian function of cultural contestation will thus supersede itself by fulfilling itself in practice—i.e. in specific places and periods of time, within the context of an urban topology, and in terms of a new attitude toward productivity. The alternative is failure.

It is possible that this analysis overlooks important aspects of the events and the situation.

14. Alternative or Alibi?

Certain alternatives that at one time seemed relevant options and dilemmas appear obsolete today. Reform or revolution, for instance. It has frequently been demonstrated that a revolution consists of an aggregate of reforms which have an overall goal and result: to dispossess the ruling class and wrest from it the ownership of the means of production and management—direct or through intermediaries—of the entire society. It has been demonstrated that there are revolutionary reforms, and that every significant reform strikes at the structures of society—the social relations of production and property.

Does a choice have to be made between the sudden and gradual approaches, between rupture and constructive activity, between violent assault and activity within the institutions? There is no theoretical reason for abandoning Lenin's strategic principles. Possibilities for action must be seized and unified in a dialectical manner. A given political attitude based on the notion of a final assault may, unexpectedly, contribute to institutional and ideological crisis—and disintegration—within the established society. An initially reformist attitude attempting to achieve no more than the reform of an institution such as the university may become transformed into extremely effective and revolutionary action. This does not exclude a conjuncture in which a choice of means may become necessary. The most profound option, however, would seem to be the following: either reconstruction of society as a whole, or reconstitution of the state. Either action from below, or activities from above.

Our analysis has tried to show the dissolution of the state, a kind of withering of its power and strategic capacity—a disintegration of absolute politics. The state is seen as engaged in a self-destruction which undermines the conditions under which it functions as well as its social "base"—even though it remains solidly rooted in economic factors. Institutions and ideologies—the superstructures crowned by the absolute state—are crumbling. Will this result in the re-establishment of conditions for an absolute state, whether capitalist or state socialist? Or will an attempt be made to establish new superstructures by separating them from the superstructures of the state, which has an existence apart?

The withering of the state, which manifests itself in the form assumed by absolute politics, can be utilized for radical change, in the perspective of a redefined socialism. These are the guiding principles: generalized self-management with all the problems it raises; continuous contestation with the accompanying confusion and disorder that are conducive to a new order; establishment of a network of base-organizations that *present* (rather than represent) the interests of the groups constituting "the people"; and optimal utilization of all technological means, including the scientific processing of information. What is involved here is not a "state" but a *process* resulting in new problems that can be solved only in social practice. The alternative to this perspective involves the risk of the re-establishment, not only of economic production (as in 1945), but also of the superstructures and structures themselves, by adapting them through codes and legislation. Are we proposing a revolutionary reformism guided by a theory of overall (industrial and urban) transformation? Perhaps. The most dangerous and obsolete approach, however, is that of a reformism hiding under revolutionary rhetoric.

What is still called "the Left"—the totality of divergent attitudes with an appearance of unity, or the totality of common attitudes with an appearance of diversity—is a cause for concern. For the past few years it has acted as though it did not want to take power, or could not guarantee it, or lacked something essential. Its political leaders seemed afraid of undermining economic growth. They undoubtedly viewed the taking of power in terms of a strictly classical approach: the economic crisis begins, the opposition allows some time for the crisis to mature, then advances a program for renewed take-off, and settles down comfortably in its command posts. Such an approach is obsolete: the institutional and superstructural crisis took place in the absence of a serious economic depression (even though there were symptoms of a depression, such as unemployment, sectors in which growth was slowing down, etc.). Can this Left take power? Certainly. But it is ill-prepared and knows it only too well, with the exception of a few personalities. What has "the Left" proposed in recent years? It has made the same proposals as the government. The difference is that "the Left" proposes to do more and do it better—better rate of growth, better distribution of the national income, etc. It has not advanced a single new conception or stimulating image of society or the state. Its prevailing concept of socialism is still that of state socialism with all of its defects (which include dreadful boredom, and an appalling lack of vitality, imagination, and social "creativity"!). In going to the bottom of things, as the saying goes, it is apparent that "the Left" wants to act and that it is moving, but it does not quite know what it wants or in what direction it is moving. Like the state power, it has crushed democracy at the base and eliminated all mediations. Weak without a bureaucratic machine and strong with a bureaucratic machine, the Left is situated on the very terrain of those with whom it is engaged in combat.

An aggregate of demands and proposals does not constitute a totality, a revolutionary program. It is neither a political "subject," nor an object, nor anything better. Trade-union practice and political practice as such are also *reduced* and *reductive.* What is lacking? A "point of view" which precisely cannot be reduced to a partial point of view and cannot reduce all-inclusiveness to the partial. The Whole? Totality? It is not a generalized individual identified with an institution, a state, or a bureaucratic machine. Such attitudes contribute neither an overall conception nor a definition of a goal. They do not provide direction. Totality, devoid of all totalitarian elements, can be viewed only as a *process* moving in the direction of the reconstruction of society on a new (industrial and urban) base.

15. Old and New Contradictions: Theses and Hypotheses.

Recent history is marked by old contradictions that have been poorly resolved or even become sharpened. There is a crucial contradiction between private ownership of the means of production, their management in the interests of a class, and the social (collective) character of production. Far from disappearing, this contradiction has assumed new forms. The state has been consolidated in appearance only. It has taken on economic and social functions, but has not ceased to establish its power above the entire society (absolute strategy and politics).

The following are a few *elementary* observations on the new contradictions. In the first place, a society established on the level reached by the productive forces tends toward over-organization, planning-oriented rationality, bureaucratic hierarchization. This tendency cannot result in cohesion; but it is real and becomes more prevalent as a result of techno-cratic processing of information. It was (and still is) very difficult in this society to maintain a *competitive sector* devoted to knowledge (scholars and others). It will be readily understood that such a sector holds great interest for those who possess economic, ideological, and political power. In this competitive sector there are struggles as to who can serve them best. Learning is produced for their use. Individuals as well as groups find themselves in conflict. Can these disputes be institutionalized? Certainly, but this entails risks.

The organization of intellectual production (production of goods, intellectual works, and men) does not prevent the survival of obsolete forms of competition such as examinations and contests that are relics of a pre-capitalist and pre-industrial past. These constitute a significant part of the intellectual heritage. The situation becomes even more intolerable as the production of intellectual skills comes to assume increasing importance throughout society. Those who are compelled to compete with one another for the profit of managers and decision-makers will eventually revolt. The situation has provoked a world-wide rebellion of intellectuals and especially students. The reduction of so-called "cultural" works to the level of commercially exploitable material products cannot fail to aggravate the explosiveness of the situation.

The students—apart from a family situation which plays a role but does not condition the group or its class structure—have nothing to sell but their labor power. This labor power, which is only potential in the case of students, is available only for a specific kind of production and a specific market. What are the consequences of these facts? Many students feel solidarity with the working class. But they also understand better than do individual workers how the repressive mechanisms of society function. As for the conflict between intellectual competition and its social use (between the exchange value of the intellectual product and its use value), the students have grasped it before the intellectuals already engaged in professions and careers. In coming to grips with these specific problems, their contestation reached an all-inclusive level. We have already referred to this phenomenon. We are now concerned with its causes. A marginal group—the intellectual producers—established in this marginal condition finds itself faced with an essential, crucial, productive task—the production of bodies of knowledge. Their situation is one of conflict, and is expressed through generalized contestation.

This crucial situation reveals still other conflicts. A conflict between integration and segregation, which affects all social categories. A conflict between the desire to participate actively in production in the broad sense (the production of intellectual works and social relations), and multiple dissociations—specifically the dissociation between production in the broad sense and production in the narrow sense, between productive activity and passive consumption, between everyday existence and creativity. A contradiction between (reduced-reductive) specialization and all-inclusiveness. A contradiction between paternalism and a repression often akin to terrorism. Last but not least, there is a contradiction between over-organization and a tendency toward dissolution, between the *strong points* and the *weak points* of society. A dialectical interaction is here revealed. A *strong point*—e.g. the organization of production and rationality in the enterprise—may change into a *weak point* when the context changes, as when the same rationality is applied to the organization of urban space. Inversely, a *weak point* such as culture or urban life may change into a *strong point* when centrality is established or re-established.

In a society still dominated by the planned organization of industrial production, there is a demand for "creativity" that can be provided only by *anomic* groups, i.e. groups that are both *social* and *extra-social*. Poets, artists, creative intellectuals (even on the less important level of the production of entertainments) derive their inspiration from a marginal situation. Marginal groups alone perceive and grasp society in its totality through the elaboration of significant representations. But the very society that asks them to be creative also attempts to subject them to its own norms and reduce their marginality. It wants to "socialize" them by integrating their activity into the (both real and fictitious) socialization of production—i.e. into the established framework of the dominant neo-capitalism which controls and manages the means of production. Art has always had ideological functions, and expressions of creativity have always been appropriated by the ruling classes and state power.

There are attempts to make creation *functional* and sometimes *official*. This is done by many different means: pressure, repression, seduction, compensation. Anomic groups are thus re-integrated or destroyed. The immanent law of collective creation has been forgotten. This creation emerges only when transgression becomes "normalized" within a necessarily marginal and anomic group. This phenomenon can be traced in the seventeenth century (Port-Royal, the theatrical companies, the learned societies), in the eighteenth century (the Encyclopedists, the critique of religion), in the nineteenth century (Romanticism), and in the twentieth century (surrealism, Marxism, etc.). It is under these conditions that a group contributes overall representations, promotes change, and tends to liquidate the past and portend the future in symptomatic works. A society that fails to take this into account will crush this famous "creativity." This gives rise to boredom and rebellion by those who feel oppressed. How should such groups be treated? This is one of the problems connected with urban life that cannot be grasped by proponents of programmed industrial organization.

This situation leads to a profound contradiction between social reality (division of labor, market, organization of industrial production) supported by ideologies that pretend not to be ideologies (economism and the theory of growth, technologism and a certain "scientificity") and ideologies that promote values considered essential to the society (patriotism, nationalism, military and political "values," classical humanism, religion, esthetics, representations of happiness, etc.). These are clearly ideologies and become discredited as such. They are dated—they emerged prior to industrialization and industrial rationality. But they are the very ideologies that provide motivation, stimulation, justification and legitimacy.

An *urban* society bases its forms and superstructures on the superstructures (institutions, ideologies) of the industrial epoch erected on determined structures and relations of production. In the recent past, new superstructures based on institutions and ideologies reflecting agricultural production have emerged within the historically conditioned framework and social relations of competitive capitalism. This represents painful labor, difficult birth, distortions and imbalances, and is governed by a law that we have already stressed. The superstructures associated with industrialization are crumbling even before earlier superstructures could be fully adapted.

The university is a typical example of a dated superstructure which originated in the pre-industrial and pre-capitalist epoch. It survived because of the strong unity between institution and ideology, but it is now lagging. Attempts are being made to overcome this lag. The university is now being viewed in terms of industrial enterprise, but this is happening at the very time it is besieged by the new problems of urban society. It used to be a marginal institution, but the transformations of society have pushed it to the forefront. The very existence of the university is today at stake. It has a social function which is chiefly pedagogic; it is a center for the production of knowledge, ideas, and people. Can it maintain itself by trying to uphold universality? What kind of university does this involve? Either the university will split, in terms of the specialized needs of the divisions of labor and the market, into separate, autonomous, and technicized institutes, with the optimal perspective of permanent education—or it will be reconstructed within an overall perspective that will raise universality to a higher and more concrete level.

In spite of the contradictions of capitalist and neo-capitalist society, industrial praxis tends toward an unattainable rational coherence. The established power, which utilizes effective rationality in this society, tries to achieve the convergence of these fragmented elements. Rationality consists of activities that are fragmented, specialized—therefore reduced and reductive in relation to the totality of society and its development. There is a tendency toward the unification of the rationalities of industry, state management, and planning, the processing of information, and scientific knowledge (concerning nature and society). This industrial practice, from Saint-Simon to the theoreticians of "industrial society," has been regarded as a fully accomplished rationality. But the attempt to unify fragmentary actions—especially very effective ones—raises problems. Marx has refuted the simplistic model of the theoreticians of industrial rationalism, by showing that coherence and totality can be achieved only after the conflicts and contradictions that are characteristic of capitalism have been resolved (these contradictions can be defined and grasped in their totality, but only by means of dialectical thought and a revolutionary critique).

For the past half-century both neo-capitalism and socialism have invoked the name of Marx. Both aim at the achievement of a fully developed rationality and coherent system on the material basis of industrial organization and planning (the level attained by the productive forces makes it possible to organize them on an all-inclusive social scale). Both sides, however, have to contend with new contradictions. These arise *unevenly* and *specifically* in terms of social and political structures, the level of productive forces and industrialization, the relations of production, and ideologies. These new contradictions are provoked partly but increasingly by urbanization.

The cohesion of societies based on industrialization therefore can be maintained only by an incoherent mixture of ideology and violence, pressure and repression. The authoritarian actions of the state cannot resolve either old or new contradictions; they try to evade their impact by *reducing* problems and possibilities. By utilizing for this irrational end specialized—i.e. reduced and reductive—activities, political action pretending to totality becomes itself reduced and reductive. This gives rise to new contradictions. A limited rationality generates its own characteristic irrationality, and this at the very moment when it proclaims itself fully developed. Every specialized (reduced and reductive) activity, including so-called philosophic or political activity, is situated in a context of pseudo-totality and false coherence, and is the object of false consciousness; these are all maintained by the established power—i.e. by repression. Learning and culture cannot overcome this incoherence, nor can they mask the situation. They are part of it; they become lost and dissolved in it.

Let us now examine the process of growth of the productive forces. It is a quantitative and relatively continuous process that passes through the relative discontinuity of structures (production and property relations) and superstructures(elaborate codifications, various ideologies and institutions). This process induces certain consequences, among which urban phenomena assume special importance. Initially a subordinate aspect of social development, these phenomena have become predominant. This raises qualitative problems that cannot be reduced to quantities of material products, space, and time. The long periods characterized by agricultural production, rural life, and agrarian (peasant) ideologies were succeeded by the industrial period with all its implications. Many regard this period as decisive and definitive; in any event the urban period has begun. The purpose and meaning of dialectical analysis is to distinguish in the overall process differences, interactions and conflicts, transitions, regressions and pauses, leaps, etc.

A new *praxis* has emerged—urban practice. It envelops yet also transforms the industrial praxis which tried, and still tries, to establish itself in a coherent and compelling manner. Clearing the way for urban praxis requires a radical critique of the ideologies and institutions associated with previous periods. Industrialization in particular can no longer be regarded as more than a transition, a historical intermediary, a "mutation" which was viewed, or which some pretended to view, as absolute. The situation therefore requires a refutation of the theories which formally reflect industrial growth—economism as well as humanism, quantification as well as the traditionalism which, in its own way, wants to destroy the machine. Urban practice and theory cannot as yet be clearly distinguished from industrial practice and the theories associated with it. This confusion enables latent or brutal repression to try to stifle the emerging practice and theory. It attempts to do so particularly by imposing an ideology that tries to mask its ideological character. A reformed university could play such a role. Its supposed adaptation to modernity, however, would merely accentuate a repressive function identified with pedagogic and cultural functions.

Among the apparently non-ideological ideologies *urbanism* requires special emphasis. Urban problems extend far beyond urbanism, in spite of the confusion between these terms. Urbanism as an ideology has little coherence and finds itself in a somewhat ambiguous situation. It relates to classical humanism as well as modernism and technocratic economism. It depends on specialized and centralized institutions supported by the state and associated with specialized activities that are integrated into the general process. Urbanism also tries to adapt representations, some of which date from the period when agricultural production prevailed (village, community, Greek or medieval city), while others date from the period of competitive or monopoly capitalism (functionalism). Urbanism tries to adapt these representations by stressing urbanization and minimizing urban praxis and its concrete problems. It cannot consequently be defined as a scientific theory, nor can it define urban rationality. It masks or mutilates urban praxis. It must, however, be allowed to develop. A revolution in theory presupposes a radical critique of urbanism as an ideological and institutional superstructure that is anterior or exterior to urban problems, and as an obstacle to emerging urban practice and the analytical or comprehensive study of this practice.

Industrial praxis became established through a (never completed) totalization of partial practices—industrial organization, planning, programming, allocation of resources, etc. Although they tend to totality, these aspects and modalities of industrial rationality have developed unevenly, and not as the expression of a pre-established reason. The law of uneven development applies, in keeping with social and political structures.

The elaboration of an industrial rationality—a superstructure elaborated on a determined base—has not yet been achieved, but it is already inadequate. The establishment of urban praxis begins with partial practices that cannot be dissociated; it involves the study of centrality and marginality, urban celebration and urban guerrilla warfare, everyday existence with its gestures and modes of behavior as well as transgressions, *anomie* and normality, topicality and utopia, playfulness and seriousness, demands and contestation, groups, classes, class strategies, etc. In brief, theory has the immense task of elaborating the elements of practice, preventing dissociations, and unifying these elements. The theoretical revolution which Marx initiated by laying bare the process of industrialization and industrial practice continues.

The theoretical revolution presupposes and implies a radical critique of the established superstructures; but this critique must not be confined to this negative role, for it also has the task of elaborating a "positive"—i.e. comprehensive—theory that gives meaning to history and events. Among the superstructures that must be subjected to a radical critique, the following may be listed: the state and specialized political machines, ideologies appearing as non-ideological, the incoherent universality of philosophy, the ideology of growth (economism), and urbanism as a product of substitution—in brief, the limited expressions of rationality.

The specialists most inclined to regard themselves unreservedly as scholars never fail to invoke rationality. But rationality viewed outside a context and as absolute becomes mutilated and rigid. The following outline of the successive expressions of reason will provide background for this crucial controversy: *Logical reason* formulated by Greek thought (Aristotle) was followed by *analytical reason* (Descartes and European philosophy), and then by *dialectical reason* (Hegel and Marx, and subsequently by contemporary inquiry). Each of these expressions integrated the preceding ones without destroying them; but this integration gives rise to problems. Similarly, *philosophical reason* as elaborated by Western tradition was followed by *industrial* practical reason (Saint-Simon, Marx, etc.) which emerging *urban ra-*

tionality is trying to supersede in our own time. On a level which is no longer mental but social, the rationality of *opinion* has given way to a rationality of *organization* which is compelled to raise questions relating to finality and meaning, in terms of a rationality of achievement. On the level of finality, *abstract humanism* (liberal and classical) was unable to maintain itself as an ideology without becoming permeated by *critical humanism*—which in turn gave rise to a concrete, practical, developed humanism. The first stage of humanism is marked by the representation of man, the abstract project of man as presented and represented by the philosophers. The second stage of humanism is marked by a fundamental contestation of purpose and meaning. The third stage is marked by the elaboration of the conception of a (finished, relative, yet "total") fullness and the will to achieve it.

Recent events have witnessed the breakdown of a certain conception of *learning*. This result of contestation should be carefully noted. Contestation struck a decisive blow at the form assumed by this learning, its content, and the conditions under which it is transmitted. Its collapse is also that of a certain rationality, which is disintegrating like the other superstructures of this society. What is involved here is not a "superstructure" in the vulgar sense of the term—i.e. a mere reflection of the "base" and structures, or a mere level in a structure. Knowledge today emerges and has an impact at all levels of social reality, from base to top. This represents a simultaneous challenge to the hierarchization of the possessors of learning, the departmentalization which underlies this fixed hierarchy, and the hierarchization of learning itself (successive ritual initiations, revelation of the esoteric and of fictitious secrets).

Self-management of all sources of *production* (to be understood in the broad sense of social production) implies self-management of learning—this is a particular but conspicuous case of self-management viewed as a pedagogy of the totality of social life. This is the only way in which it is possible to strike a decisive blow at the capitalist and bourgeois conception of knowledge—i.e. the accumulation and management of knowledge as though it were a form of capital. It goes without saying that this involves enormous problems, the solution of which requires a fresh approach to "creativity." What has to be abolished or transcended is primarily a view of learning as commodity and exchange value, characteristic of the world of commerce and commodities—it views learning as a product that can be packaged and sold. This may be a utopia. It may be a possibility which is impossible to realize. But change implies the pursuit of possibilities. What is impossible today becomes possible tomorrow.

A new rationality is emerging within the framework of a higher unity characterized essentially by increasing political awareness and understanding. This requires and implies a critique—and at best a self-critique—of absolute politics and all the ideologies that support and justify absolute politics. Political awareness and understanding alone can unify the dimensions and levels of reality and knowledge. These become reintegrated or integrated by a rationality which condenses everything man has learned about history, including the history of philosophy, knowledge, ideologies, and the state. Such a task can be undertaken only by a collective theoretical and practical effort.

16. The Twofold Status of Knowledge (Social and Theoretical)

The May 1968 events make it possible to gain a better understanding of the nature of a cultural revolution in a country that has its own specific characteristics (high level of technology, knowledge and productive forces). The cultural revolution is not limited to culture. To the extent that fictitious or real culture has a political scope, revolution arises out of the realm of politics and leads back to it—but without sidestepping the economic realm. How could it be otherwise in a country in which the myth and power of the concept of *absolute politics* prevail?

Under the sway of this concept—and in opposition to it—everything becomes political, especially what is called "culture." In this context culture becomes a means and disintegrates. The terms "culture" and "cultural" represent a jumbled mixture of art and science, ethics and esthetics, established "values" and crumbling ideologies, fictitious ends and means that are effective or believed to be effective. Knowledge itself begins to disintegrate; it becomes reduced to a mass of fragments connected by ideology and maintained by authority. This culture resembles a mosaic, but a poorly assembled mosaic showing nothing but incomplete and grimacing figures. The real situation of culture is being revealed; the cultural revolution can be defined primarily in terms of this revelation. Counterrevolutionaries would have it that revolutionaries destroy culture and order, whereas in fact it is they who reveal the dissolution of culture and the arbitrariness of order.

In its second aspect the cultural revolution shakes up the cultural institutions and ideologies which, under cover of the political regime, give a fictitious unity to "culture." In its third aspect it challenges the *social status* of knowledge; this necessarily involves raising the question of the *theoretical status* (or *epistemological status*) of specialized knowledge. One implies the other. The definition of knowledge as such implies a definition of its social functions. Inversely, a critical examination of these functions involves a determination of the proper status, forms, and (relative) autonomy of knowledge.

All those who have taken an interest in this problem will recall the discussions of knowledge, its "nature" and "essence," and the historical and social role attributed to it by Marx and Marxist thinkers. Can knowledge be defined as a *superstructure?* In one sense the answer is *yes*, for knowledge was long linked with philosophy and ideology—and these are undeniably superstructural. In another sense the answer is *no*, for knowledge does not disappear with the "base." It is a specific entity which, at any given historical stage, absorbs everything the productive forces and social development have created. Is it proper to relate knowledge to productive forces? To be sure. But what are the true relations between them? Is there a connection between knowledge, or rather specific knowledge, and technology or the organization of labor?

Nor should we neglect social relations, their specificity, and the framework of the modes of production in different countries. Should science, like language, be made to depend on the whole of social development? But there are many languages, and the diversity and differences of specialized knowledge are not the same as those of language. What relations can be said to exist between theory (knowledge), practice (which is also diversified), and ideology (or rather multiple, disintegrating ideologies, heaps of debris abandoned along the road of history, unlike knowledge and science which have a history that is not independent but nevertheless specific)?

It will be remembered that these polemics were revived and carried to a fever pitch about twenty years ago as a result of superficial and brutally imposed "theorizing." Attempts were made to counterpose *proletarian science* to *bourgeois science*. The dogmatism of the Stalinist era was thus compromised from the very outset of its (apparently) very ambitious undertaking. What was really involved, however, was a diversion designed to hide something else. The truth or falsity of the theory had little importance. At that time an ideology akin to the concept of absolute politics already tried to permeate thought through the intermediary of "culture."

It was extremely absurd to try to make logic depend on any one "social" science. It is logically inconceivable that formal logic could develop as a superstructure, and arise and disappear in terms of a "base." Once *formulated* (under historical conditions that must be explored), it remains constant. It becomes more refined but does not disappear. For more than twenty centuries formal logic has been a stable, transparent, and empty form of knowledge. As for dialectical thought and method, they do not depend on a mode of production or an economic and social "base." History, however, is not idle. It invalidates or confirms the constructs of dialectical logic and methodology, and associated concepts and theories. The *level* attained by productive forces, social development, class structure, and political superstructures may play an important role. Language may favor or inhibit dialectical thought.

There are in fact complex relations between form and content, identity and diversity, unity and conflict. Content, diversity, and conflict may to some extent be reduced or eliminated from consciousness. A particular "social" or "human" science such as sociology may incorporate an enormous ideological content and therefore be used as a political instrument. This does not exclude the fact that such an ideology may represent certain types of knowledge or pose genuine problems. To take another example, what is "urbanism"? It is nothing more than an ideology which was elaborated in France by the state apparatus and a specialized bureaucracy, and utilized for the benefit of private interests or interpreted in terms of earlier ideologies (humanism). This ideology, however, corresponds to a whole range of very real problems —those of an emerging urban society—which this ideology dissimulates and veils. Urbanism, which pretends to rationality, also has practical applications. It is a distorted and distorting expression of an uncertain and as yet undeveloped urban practice.

The cultural revolution brings all these situations to light. It forcefully raises the question of the problematical nature of specialized knowledge as a privileged instance of the concrete problems posed by society as a whole—the state, city and country, everyday existence. Specialized knowledge is transmitted in an authoritarian manner and managed bureaucratically. It provides a justification for the social hierarchy and is therefore interpreted and mutilated; but this does not make it any the less real. Bureaucracy is based on the possession and transmission—in keeping with its own set of rules and norms—of specialized knowledge. But the chief problem here is to liberate knowledge, to separate specialized knowledge without destroying it. How should these highly complex relations between the functions, forms, and structures of knowledge be analyzed? How can they be modified in terms of greater coherence and a higher rationality?

A certain analogy—quite obvious today—can be made between *capital* and *knowledge*. This analogy should not be pushed too far. Three levels of production must be distinguished. Such an analysis of course is an extension of philosophy and its concept of "totality," but it applies in a new manner. One might speak of the "three dimensions" of productive activity, were it not for the fact that this expression wrongly separates what it is supposed to join. These levels or dimensions can be distinguished as follows: production and reproduction of commodities, reproduction and production of social relations, production of intellectual works. Knowledge relates to the last of these levels; it cannot be made to depend exclusively on material production.

Insofar as it is a non-material yet socially necessary form of production, intellectual labor has specific characteristics. Knowledge, however, accumulates and becomes "capitalized" in the same manner as the material wealth represented by objects or money. It may or may not find favorable conditions for reproduction and increased accumulation. Acquired knowledge results from past labor. This is also true of capital —the accumulated wealth which bourgeois possession and management counterpose to living labor, the labor of the "collective worker," without which this wealth cannot be animated and activated. Knowledge as well is only an accumulation of dead things without continuous investigation and practical activity, without relevant labor, without a living context that can assimilate it. Constant capital acquired and owned by a class and managed in its interest is counterposed, in material as well as non-material production, to variable capital, to wage-earning creative activity. This dissimulates "social reality"—i.e. the production and reproduction of social relations and the structures making for dependence, privation, disfranchisement of labor living on past labor, absence of links between (social) collective labor and (private) ownership of the means of production.

Accumulated knowledge has been subjected—not without becoming fragmented—to the technological division of labor, and has become crystallized institutionally, in keeping with the norms of the social division of labor. This sanctions the inequality of functions, since the privileged and hierarchized functions (ownership, management) are superposed on genuine functions which become themselves hierarchized (education, transmission, investigation, assimilation, application). The technological division of scientific labor gives rise to specialized distinct enterprises (laboratories, institutes), and therefore to compartmentalization. This in no way presents an obstacle to the activities of general, bureaucratic institutions that manage this entire network in keeping with the needs of bourgeois society and with the distribution of resources in terms of the compulsions and requirements of this society.

At this point our analysis touches on the level of *superstructure*. Knowledge as such cannot be reduced to a superstructure. Ideologies and "cultural" institutions are superstructures; so are the ideological elements of specialized knowledge that date from the medieval and agrarian period: an inclination toward the secret and sacred, mystification of learning, esotericism sanctioned and concealed by jargon, confusion of practical apprenticeship and initiation, inadequate distinction between pedagogic practice and ritualization.

This agrarian and medieval ideology is alloyed with an

ideology dating from the industrial era which justifies and reinforces specialization—i.e. it legitimizes and expresses the social division of labor—firmly grafted upon a dynamic, forever provisional, and changing technological division of labor. Through this extremely confused mixture, knowledge reverts to (social) practice. It becomes increasingly absorbed by the production of things, by the production and reproduction of relations. It tends toward a unity which would integrate it. Inversely, it is (contesting, revolutionary) practice alone that has pointed up this mixture, revealed the situation, and provoked the collapse of an incoherent construct in the name of rational coherence.

How does knowledge relate to the class character of the established society? Knowledge as such is not class knowledge; this is a leftist view. And yet there *is* a connection between knowledge and the class structure of (capitalist, bourgeois) society. Knowledge is *marked* by the ruling class, particularly by the interaction "ideology-knowledge"—the term "interaction" indicating both ambiguity and contradiction. Knowledge is also the property of this class; it is transmitted according to criteria that favor this class. It is *administered*—i.e. institutionalized—by this class. It is not therefore class knowledge in the sense that the class constituted into a (historical and social) *subject* controls learning as content or object, by investing it with subjective characteristics. It is a knowledge that is inserted into class relations and their conflicts, but it provokes other specific conflicts. Viewed in this light, i.e. specifically and rationally, knowledge does not depend on a *subject*, whether social (bourgeoisie, proletariat) or political (party or state). It has content and appropriate functions, and finds formal expression (especially that of logic) according to a structural process still to be determined.

Both the social and theoretical status of knowledge are thus determined. Detached from subjectivity (that of a group as well as a class or the entire society) and disengaged from objectivism (existence conceived in terms of analogy with the existence of an object), it becomes a specific part of the contradictions of society. This also means that it gives rise to specific contradictions. The basic contradiction within the framework of (competitive or monopoly) capitalism, between private ownership of the means of production and the social character of productive labor, has specific repercussions on knowledge. This contradiction plays an extremely important role, not only because it generates actual or potential conflicts in this society, but also because it constitutes an obstacle to (economic) growth and especially to (social, qualitative) development.

Knowledge is characterized by a conflict between private ownership of specialized knowledge and the means of producing knowledge, and the social character of knowledge—i.e. the social character of productive and creative labor, applications, knowledge worthy of being pursued both for its own sake and as a practical instrument. This situation presents a specific obstacle to growth (extension of specialized knowledge, dissemination through educational practice) and qualitative development (refined pedagogy, achievement of a higher rationality).

Why did so profound a conflict, so important in terms of its implications and consequences, not come to light? Why did it fail to arouse the greatest possible concern? How was it possible to find satisfaction in a proposal for "reforms" confined to an institutional level? For what reasons? The conflict was veiled by *mediations*—ideological mediations (philosophy, morality and "values," art, esthetics, and estheticism) and institutional mediations (the university, the church, professional and functional specialized groups such as newscasters, the entrepreneurs of entertainment, etc.). These groups performed a number of functions. They legitimized a fictitious unity of "culture" while functioning in a specific "cultural" sector. But these mediations have ceased to operate in such a capacity; they were corroded and emptied of their content by absolute politics and state power; the case of the newscasters in this connection is significant. We have already stressed this fact. The events simply brought to light the latent and veiled elements and aspects of the situation. The collapse of the mediations revealed a long process of disintegration. The pretended or real lag of so-called cultural institutions can no longer veil the basic conflict centering on the "essence" of knowledge and its twofold social and theoretical status.

The reconstruction of specialized knowledge has become an important problem. Knowledge must be reconstituted, and its expropriators expropriated. The theoretical revolution—or "cultural revolution"—implies new theoretical elaborations. The unitary and comprehensive character of knowledge can no longer be viewed in terms of Encyclopedism (which dates from the pre-industrial era) or on the model of compartmentalized knowledge and an aggregate of fragments loosely held together by a narrow rationalist ideology (dating from the era of industrialism, organizational capitalism, and centralized state management). The theoretical, practical, conceptual, and pedagogic reconstruction of knowledge calls for the elaboration of a new kind of comprehensiveness—i.e. rationality.

It should be emphasized that such a rationality has a twofold character. It is both historical and theoretical, it arises out of practice but must be conceptually and methodologically (epistemologically) elaborated. The formalization of learning and the determination of its epistemological status, however, are, in themselves and in terms of their end and purpose, of no interest. These theoretical elaborations are meaningful only if they *serve* the practical and effective transformation of knowledge, its management and practical transmission. The propagation of specialized knowledge requires continuously renewed actualization and enrichment. It constitutes a partial practice—the practice of pedagogy—inserted, coherently or incoherently, in a total practice. These observations are themselves part of the theoretical revolution.

A model should perhaps be proposed at this point. It should be noted that philosophical concepts (subject and object viewed in their unity and conflicting relations, and absolute system and coherence) are no longer adequate. The crux of the matter lies in the relations between form and content. The real (material) pole is marked by "nature." The rational (formal) pole is marked by logic—a logic which is perfectible and therefore not static, but transparent due to the absence of content. Dialectical logic invests the relations between *form* and *content* with concepts and language. "Pure" and "empty" logic becomes the center of a constellation of demarcated forms that constitute a structure; however, each one preserves a specific content (mathematical form, forms of exchange and communication, juridical form, urban form, etc.). This implies a degree of relativism and pluralism, but without separate substantialities. Metaphysical thought gave autonomous substance to form, content, their relations, nature, and the logic of identity. But this alienated—alienating mode of thought is no longer relevant. Social practice (praxis) perpetually establishes and re-establishes a dialectical unity between material nature and logical forms. A distinction can be made between critical reflection (a permanent characteristic of knowledge) and ("positive" and constructive) theoretical elaboration—but such a distinction must never become a break. The negative and positive aspects of thought are as inseparable as theory and practice, or ideology and specialized knowledge.

The last two questions are still unresolved. The range of concrete problems does not constitute an absolute entity that unifies the rational and the real once for all. It incorporates problems that are not empirical but based on practice. These problems are not unrelated, but the connections between them cannot be uncovered formally. The unity which makes it possible to speak of a set of problems is revealed in and through the practical activity that creates (or produces) it, but with the aid of theoretical reflection which uncovers and then redistributes the elements of specialized knowledge. This set of problems implies the ambiguity of ideology and specialized knowledge as well as the differences between them.

Can we speak of pure, absolute knowledge purified of all ideological admixtures? The answer is affirmative, for at best formal logic is such knowledge—it is "pure" because it is transparent and devoid of content. But the answer is also negative, as far as concrete knowledge linked to a content and practice is concerned. There is no body of specialized knowledge that may not eventually be revealed as a mixture of ideology and knowledge. Is there an absolute theoretical criterion that makes it possible to demarcate them with certainty? No. "Pure" logic alone can claim to be able to provide such a criterion, but this claim exceeds its rights. Theoretical work aiming at the separation of ideology and knowledge can never be considered definitive. Critical and self-critical labor —a negative approach linked with a positive and constructive approach—can cease only when specialized knowledge is completed, i.e. when the unity of the rational and the real has been achieved. This unity delineates the horizon of knowledge, but it is infinitely remote and cannot be reached.

Ideology arises out of a practice and returns, or tries to return, to practice. In this sense it is possible to speak of "ideological practice." Practice, however, belies ideology, and it is in this sense that there is a "criterion of practice." The danger exists that the concept of "ideological practice" may dissimulate the practical failure of all ideologies. "Ideological practice," moreover, corresponds to reactionary, counterrevolutionary practice. Urbanism, for example, an ideology of the centralized state, is characterized by a twofold failure: its applications are revealed as monstrously incoherent, and it obstructs the development and awareness of urban practice. Its "inhuman" character is but an additional element of a basic failure.

The concept of "theoretical practice" has a limited scope of validity. Viewed absolutely, it may dissimulate the practical origin of all theories. It would undoubtedly be more valid to make a distinction between *partial practice* and *all-inclusive practice,* and reserve for the latter the traditional Marxist term of *praxis.* We have very briefly indicated how the *praxis* (all-inclusive practice) of the industrial era emerged from partial practices through accumulation rather than rational totalization. This accounts for the fact that this praxis is characterized by a *limited rationality* (it has irrational implications and is maintained by a repressive power). Ideology endows lmited rationality with an absolute character, extrapolates from partial practices, and veils the limitations of this rationality.

The *urban praxis* projected earlier would, in keeping with the hypothesis we have adopted, become established through a coherent *totalization* of partial practices (including those of the industrial age, freed from extrapolation, pressure and repression). Inasmuch as theory influences the formation of urban praxis, it is and will be possible to speak of "theoretical practice." This theoretical practice, however, cannot be clearly distinguished from revolutionary practice. But such a clear distinction becomes unnecessary once "revolution" is no longer confused with violence but comes to be identified with the transformation of the existing world, in keeping with its deepest tendencies and the desire to overcome its contradictions. Everyday practice, however, remains steeped in ambiguity. It conceals both repression and revolutionary possibilities. As for partial practices—specialized and therefore reduced-reductive (including specifically theoretical activity) —they must become the object of continuous self-criticism and reciprocal criticism in order for their limitations and divergences to be overcome. This is the only way in which totalization can be achieved—i.e. through the simultaneous formation and formulation of transformed praxis and rationality.

The unity of knowledge will certainly not be found in (empirical or rationalist) philosophy, "pure" forms, or an inviolable epistemological construction. This unity is situated historically on the level of *political awareness and understanding*. Political reflection alone makes it possible to conceive of the convergence of all modes of knowledge and partial practices, and to perceive the entire horizon of theory and practice. But this should not be misunderstood. "Political awareness" in this sense does not correspond to the political awareness of a representative of the state, and even less to that of a professional politician. On the contrary. It implies unceasing critical analysis of absolute politics and the ideologies elaborated by specialized political machines. It is in this sense and in this sense alone that political awareness can lead to the unity of knowledge and the highest rationality. Viewed on a different level, the term "political" is restored to its oldest meaning—the theoretical and practical knowledge of social life in the community. Society and community in fact achieve, on an altogether different level, a new unity within urban society.

This model makes it possible to examine and perhaps to specify both the social (and political) status of knowledge and its theoretical (epistemological) status. In terms of this model, knowledge is made to depend neither on a specific object, an object in general, a specific subject, a subject in general, a system viewed absolutely, nor on the systematized notion of a "corpus" of specialized knowledge. But knowledge is not suspended in a void; it must be legitimized or justified. Rationality has a historical foundation and social props. Historical materialism and continuous dialectical elaboration must be integrated in the model. The dominant polarity of (material) nature and (logical) form provide a framework for the whole—a whole which contains and defines forms, functions, and the structures of learning, without any one of these concepts reducing the others to a minor, passive, and subordinate role.

An educator cannot, any more than an engineer or a technician, be considered a villain or a public enemy. What we are witnessing is the collapse of an ideology of hierarchization, a representation of an order which places the teacher above the taught, the ruler above the ruled, knowledge above an ignorance in search of learning and in the process of acquiring it. It is consequently an ideology of initiation and esotericism, and fragmented specialization deprived of totality—one which believes and considers itself superior. Classical philosophy in this connection contributes clarity with its inherent twofold thesis, long since dissipated, of learned ignorance and the Socratic method of eliciting people's ideas. This twofold thesis must be restored and integrated under new conditions, as must all the theses of philosophy.

An educator is certainly not an "engineer of souls." He does not fashion souls in terms of acquired and fixed learning. He is an individual. An engineer may or may not be talented; a physician may or may not be gifted, perspicacious, or inspired. Does the educator have no other task than to transmit formal learning and communicate partial bodies of knowledge? Should his abilities and talents be confined to pedagogy in view of the fact that the practice of pedagogy also demands ability and talent, and pedagogic originality requires genius? The conception of education as a reflection, refraction, or diffraction of prior learning to be merely transmitted is wrong. Knowledge will not become a collective concern on all levels (from that of pupils and students to that of the entire society) if individuality is stifled. Transmission of knowledge and research cannot be successful if viewed in terms of an abstract, technocratic model for the dissemination of information. An educator is not a mere conveyer, nor is the institution called "university" a warehouse. Can knowledge be reconstructed? Yes, but not on such a model. Can there be a new rationality? Yes, but it must be radically transformed by an immense labor (education, research, discovery) which must be collective as well as individual, and which can unify these two inseparable aspects of praxis. This labor must be productive—that is, creative.

One of the great ideas of philosophy is thus re-appropriated and transformed in terms of new conditions. This idea is part of the project of philosophy, but it lost its way and was alienated. Education must not be based on the concepts of certitude or incertitude. Certitude results in dogmatism; its tendency is to move from the relative to the absolute, from partiality to totality. Incertitude leads to nihilism. Between these two there is a third way—the way of truth, which in no way resembles the political "third way," and which represents the scope and orientation of revolutionary truth. Education ought to center on concrete problems that are both practical and theoretical, both empirical and conceptual. It is not to be construed as a fixed, unchanging wall. It is not vertigo on the brink of the abyss.

We have indicated the range of concrete problems that could provide a core for an education capable of transcending the disciplines marked by excessive certitude as well as the incertitudes of the interdisciplinary approach. The dominant problems are those relating to urban society. These are becoming increasingly more important than the problems of an industrialization still in process. It goes without saying that this range of urban problems historically reflects a wider set of problems relating to "man" or rather the "human being."

This perspective restores neither rationalism nor empiricism; it has no affinity with either sociologism (even though it takes historical and social reality into account) or philosophism. The place given to logic meets certain objections and accusations, notably those of empiricism and sociologism. The importance attributed to (material) nature answers the accusations of abstract scientism and idealist philosophism. As for the thesis that political knowledge can bring about the unification of compartmentalized knowledge, it will likely continue to be attacked with the same arguments that have been used ever since philosophy and the pursuit of knowledge began.